BASALI!

BASALI!

Stories by and about women in Lesotho

Edited by

K. LIMAKATSO KENDALL

1995
UNIVERSITY OF NATAL PRESS
Pietermaritzburg

Published 1995 by University of Natal Press
Private Bag X01, Scottsville 3209, South Africa

ISBN 0 86980 918 0

Cover design: David Langmead, from a photograph
by K. Limakatso Kendall

Typeset in the University of Natal Press
Printed by Kohler Carton and Print
Box 955, Pinetown 3600, South AFrica

Contents

Acknowledgements

It was my sister in the spirit, Tess Onwueme, who first sent me to Africa, and for that I shall be endlessly grateful. The Fulbright Foundation of the U.S.A. paid for my two years in Lesotho, and Judy Butterman, of the United States Information Service, eagerly supported my attempt to find Basotho women writers and provided space for one writers' group to take place. I'm also grateful for the encouragement and friendship of Chris Dunton, Chair of the English Department at the National University of Lesotho for most of the time while I was preparing this anthology. Mafina Mphuthing, now Registrar of that university, and Caroline Madibeng, of the English Department, answered questions, provided translations and proper spellings of Sesotho words, and were good-humoured and patient advisers; the work could not have matured without them. Moroesi Akhionbare made the Maseru writers' group possible and contributed to my life and work in Lesotho with wry humour and excellent good sense. Gisela Prasad, Matseliso Mapetla, Hopolang Phororo, and Janet Nyeko all read the stories and formed a cheering-section for the book-to-be. Julia Chere-Masopha, my surrogate-daughter, contributed to the book with her loving belief in it and helpful problem-solving in many areas of my life. I thank my North American, African-American, and Mexican-American friends – especially those who helped me to develop my politics concerning orature and third world women writers.

Even with the help of all these people, the book would have remained only a dream and several years of lost effort, but for Margery Moberly, head of the University of Natal Press. Her excitement, belief, and hard work took the book out of my computer and into the world.

Grateful acknowledgement is made for permission to publish the following copyrighted material:

'Three Moments in a Marriage' © 1995 Mpho 'M'atsepo Nthunya.

'An Unexpected Daughter' © 1995 'M'amoroosi 'M'aseele Qacha.

'The Lost Sheep is Found' © 1995 Tembela Seleke.

'Give Me a Chance' © 1994 Mzamane Nhlapo. First published in *The Kalahari Review*, 1994.

'Arriving Home in a Helicopter' by Julia 'M'amatseliso Khabane. © 1995 Sr. Alina Khabane.

'How She Lost Her Eye' © 1995 Inahaneng Tsekana.

'A Letter to 'M'e' © 1995 Moroesi Akhionbare.

'Catastrophe' © 1995 Gugulethu S. Dlamini.

'The Decision to Remain' © 1995 Mapheleba Lekhetho.

'The Universe' © 1986 'M'asefinela Mphuthing. First published in the U.S.A.

'Why Blame Her?' © 1995 'M'atseleng Lentsoenyane.

'The African Goddess: The Figure in My Past' © 1995 Monica Nthabeleng Ramarothole.

'What about the *Lobola*?' by Anonymous. © 1995 Clement Matjelo.

'Escape to Manzini' © 1995 Nomakhosi Mntuyedwa.

'Ask Him to Explain' © 1995 Mpine Tente.

'How I Became an Activist' © 1995 'M'amapele Chakela. An earlier version of this story, entitled 'The Songs I Didn't Sing' was first published by the National University of Lesotho Publishing House in 1995.

'*Basali!* A Photographic Essay' © 1995 K. Limakatso Kendall.

Introduction

K. LIMAKATSO KENDALL

Basali literally translated into English is 'women', but its meaning as an exclamation in Sesotho is rich with humour, affection
and women's connection. Usually exclaimed by one woman to
another, often delivered with a laugh, an amused shaking of the
head, or a clapping of hands, *Basali!* strongly evokes Basotho
women's love and respect for one another. It is roughly equiva-
lent to 'Girl!' in African-American English and is spoken with the
same high-toned, sliding inflection. It could be translated as
some variant of 'You're so sassy/clever/good-looking/outrageous/
hilarious/dangerous/powerful/dazzling/audacious that I don't
know what more to say to you!' But note that 'Girl!' is singular
and praises individual audacity. *Basali!* is plural; it carries with
it the implication that whatever the one woman is, and is being
praised or admired for, is also true for the rest of her kind. 'You
are outrageous, powerful, etc.; and so are *we all!*'

I collected these stories while working at the National University of Lesotho as a Fulbright Scholar. Twelve stories were
written down by students in a senior seminar in English called
'Women's Writing'. We noted that very few Basotho women have
written in, or been translated into, English and we discussed the
many social and political reasons for that. We noted the many
women storytellers in our lives whose circumstances have denied
them literary 'voice.' Then we set out to elicit and collect stories
of women's lives in Lesotho.

Some of the students served as translators, collecting the
stories word for word from oral tellers ('Arriving Home in a
Helicopter' and 'What About the Lobola' for example); others
listened to the stories and then rewrote them in their own words,
striving to keep the spirit of the original teller ('How She Lost

Her Eye', and 'The Decision to Remain'). A few students were so encouraged by this process that they decided to tell their own stories ('The Lost Sheep is Found' and 'The African Goddess' are autobiographical stories).

Several stories were written by mature professional women, members of a group called 'Basotho Women in the Media' who participated in a writers' workshop I led for six months at the United States Information Service offices in Maseru. Three were written by Basotho women who were colleagues of mine at the National University of Lesotho.

In our seminars and workshops, the writers and I discussed the politics of language as described by Ngugi wa Thiong'o in *Decolonising the Mind*; we read and discussed the 'Africanised' English of Sindiwe Magona, Flora Nwapa and Ama Ata Aidoo; and we read stories in African-American English by Toni Morrison, Alice Walker, Alexis de Veaux, and Becky Birtha. We also read Gloria Anzaldua's *Borderlands* and noted that Basotho women, like their Mexican-American sisters, suffer punishment at school when caught speaking their mother tongue and are forced from childhood to live in a bilingual world in which their mother tongue is not valued as a means of literary or artistic expression.

Several students were troubled by the ethics of encouraging young Basotho writers to use non-standard English, when the ability to write and speak standard English is a survival-skill in Lesotho. Yet they were intrigued by Ngugi wa Thiong'o's idea of writing in their mother tongue and then translating their own work into English; and by the notion of creating a variant-English, as west African and African-American writers have done, which would be unique to Lesotho and therefore, in a sense, their own, and not the coloniser's English.

What most inspired the writers of these tales was the work of Mpho 'M'atsepo Nthunya, the least formally educated of the writers in this volume. She is a highly respected storyteller who dictated her autobiography to me in her own strongly 'Sesotho-ised' English. I read some of her stories in the writers' groups. The form and syntax of her language carries cultural messages, ways of looking at life specific to the Basotho people. Mzamane

Nhlapo, a former miner and himself a fine storyteller, said, *"M'e* Mpho's stories *are* Lesotho. She somehow tells the core of what life here is all about.'

Mzamane Nhlapo's mother was seriously ill when he was writing about her. He says boys in Lesotho seldom know their mothers well because the boys are sent off to herd animals and to learn the ways of men almost as soon as they are old enough to walk. Nhlapo used this writing project as a means to get to know his mother for the first time by hearing her story and finding the words to re-tell it in English.

Sr. Alina Khabane was able to deepen her bond with her sister-in-law by cajoling her into telling the whole, hilarious story of 'Arriving Home in a Helicopter'. Gugulethu Dlamini had to make numerous trips home to Durban, South Africa, to sit with her friend for the telling of 'Catastrophe'. Inahaneng Tsekana did his story-gathering during school vacations when he could travel home to the mountains around Mokhotlong to ask questions and listen to the aunt who reared him. Tembela Seleke, exiled from South Africa during apartheid, faced some of her deepest fears and most painful memories in order to tell how she dared to end her nine years of exile in Lesotho.

All of these stories are 'true', in so far as any story can be true. Certain details are selected; others left out. Actions are distorted by the eyes (and perceptions) of those who witness them. Dialogue is selectively recalled. A structure must be chosen for the telling, and that structure may demand a 'climax' or an 'ending' which is arbitrary or forced. Life is seldom so tidy or so clearly focused.

Many of the stories can only be told in multiple languages, revealing the necessity for black people in southern Africa to be multilingual. English is only one of several languages which black people must speak in order to live and find employment in southern Africa, though such is not the case for whites, who can flourish economically while only speaking their mother-tongue. The authors have included parenthetical translations for the benefit of English-speaking readers, but the record of the various languages in which dialogue takes place is vital to the tone and texture of the telling.

This collection is therefore a hybrid: a bridge, perhaps, between orature and literature. At the simplest level it is story-telling made solid in print. These stories reveal glimpses of traditional Basotho culture, with its sangomas, circumcision schools, witches, bride-prices and extended rural family life; and glimpses of a culture under pressure – families disrupted by migrant labour, women and men brutalized by apartheid in South Africa, teenagers whose western values violate their parents' expectations, and middle-class office-workers whose rural families live by a different clock than the one that ticks in Maseru.

The stories also tell much about relations between the sexes in Lesotho: love, marriage, passion, divorce, wife-beating and child-abuse are here, though, in every case, the focus of the story is the decisions women make, the actions they take to protect and to provide for themselves and their children, and, in several cases, to care for the women or the men they love. There are no passive victims here, no pitiable characters who are merely haggard survivors of ill fortune. Within the range of choices available to them, these women choose bravely and with conviction.

Rhythm is a central element of form in many of the stories, as is experimentation with tense and syntax. Even when translated into English, there is a music in lines taken from storytellers who create suspense while embroidering a story and who caution their reader-listeners 'not to hurry for the soup before the meat is cooked'. Many lines should be read aloud to be savoured fully.

Linear narrative seldom appears; rather a kind of spiralling of details builds an ethos in which a story takes place, past and present weaving together. Past tense is used while the story-teller regards the tale with some distance or reflection. As a story intensifies, the teller often shifts into present tense. Idiomatic expressions reveal modes of interpreting experience which trans-mit ways of being; and certain words or concepts which have no direct English equivalents are footnoted. A glossary of commonly-used Sesotho words appears at the end of the volume.

A word about ownership: the writers and I are deeply con-cerned about the question of whose stories these are. When a story is told with artistry in Sesotho, heard with respect, written down by the receiver, translated into English, reshaped – a paragraph moved from the end to the middle, a phrase deleted – then typed onto a computer disk, and published, whose story is it? Who should hold the copyright? What percentage of the profits, if there are any, should go to whom? How can the transcriber or translator of an oral tale avoid 'mining' or exploiting the teller of the tale? How much of the work of the telling is in the ears and heart of the person who hears and creatively translates or re-tells a story? We cannot ignore the history of white entrepreneurs swooping down on Africa and mining its richest resources for their own profit, nor of neo-colonialists imitating the original colonisers. We agreed not to publish unless each contributor (sometimes that means the translator/editor) could retain copyright to her or his own story. We agreed that in those cases where the story was first transmitted orally, the people who wrote the stories down and claimed the copyright would share any future profits or royalties with the women who told the stories; and we agreed that all contributors (including me, as 'author' of the photographic essay) would take an equal share of any future profits or royalties, and that I would take no payment for editing the anthology. The University of Natal Press, a non-profit-making organisation, endorsed all these agreements and offered fifty percent of proceeds after costs to the contributors.

K. Limakatso Kendall
July, 1995

Three Moments in a Marriage

MPHO 'M'ATSEPO NTHUNYA

The Boer Policemen Find Me

When I was a young girl in the Republic, I saw the Boer policemen in black suits with yellow shining things on the neck; black hats with a yellow patch; and black boots. They carried short, heavy sticks which they used to beat people on the head, neck, or back. I was afraid of them.

The first time I saw the policemen in the Republic was when they were catching black people and putting them in a car, kicking them and forcing them to jail. School children would talk of *Maburu* like they talk of space monsters now. Only the *Maburu* were real. They really could catch you and take you away, and for many there was no coming back. No one can count how many did not come back, because the *Maburu* didn't care about the number they have killed. They just throw the bodies in a heap behind the jail.

The police were many. One time the Basotho killed a policeman, and the white policemen brought many *Maxhosa* so they could fight the Basotho, because the Boers didn't like to fight the Basotho. They preferred to use the *Maxhosa* to fight us; they say, 'These blacks are always killing each other,' but it is they who pay us to do it. We are poor, and they offer much money. They say to the *Maxhosa*, 'The Basotho want to kill you; we are going to help you with these guns.' And they give the *Maxhosa* guns and money to come in and do their work for them. They don't care if the *Maxhosa* die.

So the Basotho killed this policeman with their *molamu* and an axe with a long handle. They say when they cut the policeman's head off, his head bounced off in one direction, his body in another direction. We knew there would be trouble after.

Other policemen came from other places; they were called to come and kill the Basotho. The Basotho ran away because there were many white men now, with guns and tear-gas, and the white policemen called many *Maxhosa* to help them. It was like an army of white men and *Maxhosa*, moving into the Location. The tear-gas was there, so the people ran away and the *Maburu* went chasing after them. Many people died, white and *Maxhosa*, because the Basotho were great fighters. Only four Basotho died. Others had to go to the hospitals.

Right after my marriage to Alexis, they came to the house where we slept. Maybe they were bored that night; they had nothing to do. So they came to beat up some black people, see what they could do to amuse themselves. They just knocked hard on the door, and they shouted at us, *'Vula! Vula!'* Open! Open! The owner of the house, who was Alexis's cousin, went and opened the door. They say, 'Permit! We want a permit!' And they check to see if every person in the house has a permit.

I didn't have a permit, because it was only right after Alexis's family took me to make me his wife. I was maybe four or five days living in that house. So when they find this, they say, *'Phuma! Hamba!'* Which we can see means I should go out. I go.

Alexis was not there; he was working night-shift at the mine. I go with the *Maburu* to the car. We were full in that car, it was like a combi; they called it a 'pick-up' because the police used it to pick up many people and take them to jail. We went to the police station. We were just like sheep there. They shouted at us, 'Come on, come on!' I got very frightened because I didn't like those policemen and I didn't know what they would do to me. Even now I have nightmares about them. If I see them I am afraid.

'Get in!' They pushed me in the jail, with many other women. I stayed there for two days. All the other women were there because they didn't have permits or they were caught selling *joala*.

They fed us *papa* with salt on it. Tea to drink with small sugar, very little sugar. It was a big room with a bucket at one end for using the toilet. You go there and relieve yourself and there is nothing to wipe with and nowhere to wash your hands. You have to eat in the same room with this bucket which everyone in the room has to use. Blankets on the floor – black blankets, very dirty. Some of the women said there were fleas and bed bugs in the blankets, but I didn't see them.

After two days there came a white policeman. He stood just at the door, looked in and shouted, 'Come on!' We don't know who he means to come on. He is just standing at the door staring at us. We are sitting. Nobody moves. It seems like nobody is breathing in this room. He doesn't call the name of a person. We wait.

Then the policeman comes, opens the door to the cell, and says to me, 'Agnes! Come out!' Agnes is my Christian name, so I come out. I don't know if maybe they are going to kill me, or what.

I find my husband outside. I sign the papers and I go, we go home. Alexis had to pay them twenty pounds. That was very much money back then. He took the money he was making from work, and he paid them. After that, I got a permit. It's like a passport, a permit to stay in that house. I didn't have one because I was not staying in that house – my permit was for my parents' house. You have to have a permit to sleep in a particular house.

They could come any time they like, come to the Location and get people – maybe men, maybe women – and beat them, shove them in the pickup, yell at them like they yell at dogs, kill them if they like.

Even now, I know these Boer policemen still pay black people to kill each other. We always hear that they are killing men in the mines. When it's a fight in the mines, and the police come in, they come not to make peace but to kill as many black men as they can. It is their sport.

When they look at you with their red eyes, it's frightening. They are jealous, always jealous of the black people. I don't know why. They don't like black people. I think about why, but I can't find any answer. They just hate us. They call us monkeys.

The second time I went to Benoni, after my first two babies died, I had a permit, everything I needed to have. I saw them passing through the streets, looking for illegal *joala*. People would dig holes in the ground and put a tank of *joala* in it, then cover it up and smear it so it looks like the floor. Put a mat over it, and nobody can know there is *joala* in this house.

When the police go in a house they take sharp sticks and they pound the floor with these sticks, looking. They break a woman's things, tear her mats, make holes in her linoleum. If they find a hidden tank of *joala*, they say 'Take this out of the ground!'

She takes it out and they put her in the pickup. If they like, they will take the *joala* with her. Sometimes they pour the *joala* all over the house and say, 'Go in the pick-up with your empty tank.'

I was never making *joala* when I lived in the Republic, but still the police would come and make holes in my mats with their sticks, looking for *joala*. When they are in my house I am shaking, shaking like a herd boy in winter, even if it is a hot day. They can do anything they like with you.

After this I tell Alexis I want to come home to Lesotho, because I don't want to see these things. So we come home to Marakabei, but I still have nightmares about these policemen. I don't want them, with their red eyes. I don't know why they have these red eyes, maybe it's the hate in them.

'M'alineo Chooses Me

When I was living in the mountains near Marakabei I got a special friend. She was living in another village, and I passed her house when I was going to church every month. One day she saw me and said, 'What is your name?'

I told her I was 'M'atsepo Nthunya. So she said, 'I always see you passing here. Today I want to talk to you. I want you to be my *motsoalle*.' This is a name we have in Sesotho for a very special friend. She says, 'I love you.' It's like when a man chooses you for a wife, except when a man chooses, it's because he wants to share the blankets with you. The woman chooses you the same way, but she wants love only. When a woman loves another woman, you see, she can love with her whole heart.

I saw how she was looking at me, and I said, '*Ke hantle.*' It's fine with me. So she kissed me, and from that day she was my *motsoalle*. She told her husband about it, and he came to my house and told my husband, and these two husbands became friends too. It was a long distance from my house to her house, and she was lonely because she had no children. It was only her and her husband. Most of the time I would only see her once a month, when I went to church. We would meet outside her house and walk to church together. She would sit by me in church, and we would hold hands. There was a café near her village, and when I went to the café, I would meet her, or if she was not around I would see a child and say, 'Go tell 'M'e 'M'alineo I'm here in the café.' Then she would come, and we would talk until it's time for me to go.

She loved me so much that she bought me a *seshoeshoe* dress and two brooms. One day my *motsoalle* said she wanted me to come to her house for a feast to celebrate our friendship. She cooked for days to get ready, and even me, I made much bread and *joala* and two chickens to add to her feast. I went to her house with five women, my husband, and two other men.

When we arrive at her house we find that she has prepared a sheep. She shows us the sheep and says, 'There is your food.' It was like a wedding.

So we say our thanks, and they take the sheep and slaughter it. We go into the house and begin singing, every one feeling happy. We sing while we wait for the meat, and those who drink *joala*, drink all day. Those who don't drink *joala* have *motoho* and Coke. So when the food is ready and the meat is cooked, then we sit down. We eat meat, bread, samp, everything we can think of. It was summer, so it was hot. We stayed the whole day. In the afternoon, around six, I kissed my *motsoalle* goodbye and we went back to our village, singing all the way. I remember it was late, about ten, when we got home, walking by foot, and when we got home we kept on singing till 2 o'clock in the morning.

As soon as light came, our neighbours arrived and began drinking what was left of the *joala*. There was much left. The only ones who don't drink are me and another lady. I never liked *joala*. My mother and father both never drank *joala*, even my brother Sephefu, we didn't like it. But we didn't mind if other people wanted it. Still, we were tired from all that walking and singing and drinking and eating meat all day.

Another time, a year later, my *motsoalle* comes for a feast at my house. So she comes with many women and many husbands carrying *joala* and *motoho*. They arrive at noon or so, and we took the whole day. When they arrived I showed them the sheep, and after that we slaughtered it and cooked it. There were many people coming for the party. All these people knew that my *motsoalle* was visiting and they came to honour us for loving each other. We brought some of the people inside the house, and the rest of the people who came for the feast stayed outside. Those inside were singing, waiting for their food. Those outside were dancing. So when we finished cooking, we put all the food on big dishes: meat in one dish, bread in another, and many drums of *joala*. I call my *motsoalle* and say, 'There is your food.'

So I stand up and feed the people inside and outside. They were dancing all day; I had a windup gramophone with two loud speakers, and I put on the music – jive records, African jive. I got the records in Maseru.

I gave her a dress my husband, Alexis, bought in Maseru, and a *doek* to match. They stayed the whole day until it was about seven, but they had to go then. They were a little drunk, and they had a long way to walk. They took *joala* in five-litre buckets to drink on the way home. So in the morning there were still some people drinking outside and inside, jiving and dancing and having a good time.

Alexis says to them, 'Oh, you must go to your houses now. The *joala* is finished.'

They said, 'We want meat.'

He gave them the empty pot to show them the meat is all gone. But the ladies who were drinking didn't care. They said, 'We are not here to see you; we are coming to see 'M'atsepo.'

They sleep, they sing, they dance. Some of them are *motsoalle* of each other. I go out to talk with them, but they are too drunk to understand. They tell me, 'We are jiving here, just wind up that gramophone so we can dance.'

I say, 'I'm tired. I need to sleep.' But I was laughing, because I was happy, and it was all feeling so nice.

After that, my *motsoalle* sometimes sends me green maize or peas if I have none. We always sit together at church. We stay very good friends. But after some years, my *motsoalle* left her husband to find work in Maseru. He was not treating her well, and they had no children, so it was hard for her to stay alone with him in the mountains.

In Maseru she could not find work. She became a drunkard. I was very sad for that. I saw her last year, on the street. She is no longer my *motsoalle* because she's drinking too much. She was ashamed when she looked at me. I met her selling *moroho* outside a store. I greeted her. I asked her, 'What's the matter with your face?' It was so swollen.

She said, 'It's because I'm poor. I'm working very hard. My husband doesn't want me anymore. Sometimes I have nothing to eat.'

I said, 'But you left your husband first.'

She said, 'Yes, because he was not sleeping at home, so I left him. But now I am tired and want to go home, but my husband married another wife.' So she is still in Maseru, and her husband is near Maseru with another woman. They have been away from the mountains a long time.

In the old days celebrations of friendship were very beautiful – men friends and women friends. Now this custom is gone. People now don't love like they did long ago.

The Snow Was So Cold It Was Blue

I know it is true that people who are sick for a long time can tell you when they are going to die. Alexis knew, right to the very hour. But his mother's death was a surprise to everyone.

In August 1961, I was in my mother's house in Roma. I had got another baby boy, and I stayed with my mother until he was three months old, when I began to pack my things to go home to the Maluti. Before I could leave my mother's house, my mother-in-law, 'M'anthunya arrived. She came to say hello to me, and to see the baby. We slept together, and she told me that I should hurry home to look after the children, because she was on her way to Maseru to find work, and there was no one home to do the cooking or look after the house. She said they were ploughing, but they had nothing to plough. There was no food in the fields that year. There was nothing to eat. That was why she had to go try to find work in Maseru.

I just took only two weeks and found myself at home with Ralibuseng on my back. The day I came home I got a message that 'M'anthunya had passed away. I could not believe it at first. They said she was sick for two days only, and then she passed. It was a shock to us, and it was a time for me to see that everything was up to me. So quickly, with no preparation, I became the woman at the head of the family.

My father-in-law went down to Maseru to bury her, but there was no funeral. We couldn't go, because it was raining. The rivers were full, and nobody could walk through them with a small child. I sat in the house, watching the rain fall, thinking many things. Alexis was the first son, so now I had to take care of all the children and the fields. My father-in-law was like another child. He couldn't do anything for himself.

I stayed in my little rondavel and left the sister and brothers of Alexis in the big house with the old man, but they all came to me for food. It was a hard time, because it was true what 'M'anthunya said to me in Roma: there was no food. There was one girl in the house, but she was too young to cook. I had four children; Alexis had two brothers still at home and one sister. Seven children, two men, and me.

For three more years we struggled. Alexis brought money home when he could. The fields improved. The sheep increased. Slowly we came to feel safe from hunger again, and then in August 1964, I got another baby boy. For this one I stayed in the Maluti, because the family could not keep going if I went home to have my baby properly. I asked an old lady living near to my house to help me for a few days. She knew how to cut the cord and do what was necessary when the baby came.

This baby was Mofihli, born 16 August 1964, while the snow was falling. There was a heavy snow that year, snow up to my hips if I walked outside. There was so much snow it was blue. When you lift your foot out of the snow, the hollow place looks blue. It was that cold. It was the same snow that brought the cold into Alexis's bones.

Alexis was driving a tractor with a snow plough in the mountains, clearing the road to the Katse Dam they were building. We called it Letsola Terai at that time. He had a blanket around his waist and over his legs, but it was not enough. He got cold inside his legs. At the end of the month he came home and said, 'The snow was falling on my legs, and my legs have started to be sore.' He told me to help him put his feet in a basin of hot water before he went to bed, and I rubbed his legs with a smelly yellow medicine he brought home. I rubbed it into his legs and wrapped his legs in big heavy socks. He arrived home on a Thursday. On Sunday he went back to work.

He worked on the snow plough again, but in only two weeks they sent him to Maseru, to the hospital. As soon as I find a letter that he is in hospital, I go right away to see him. I left the older children with Alexis's brother and took the little ones to my mother in Roma. I took only the baby on my back, and I walked to Lithabaneng, on the road to Maseru. There I found some of 'M'anthunya's relatives, and they let me spend the night; the next day I walked on into Maseru.

Alexis was in a big room with many men; they called it Ward Five. They have bandaged him in cotton wool, from his feet to his hips. He said he was feeling a little bit better. He stayed in hospital six weeks. I used to go visit him every Friday and Saturday. On Sunday I would walk back to Roma to take care of the children.

After six weeks, Alexis came out of hospital and went to Lithabaneng for a week; then he went back to work. It was no more cold, but his body was feeling cold. It was October; it was spring. But he was cold, and I worried about that. Nothing would make him warm. He said the cold was deep in the bones of his legs.

I went home to the Maluti to look after all the children, the sheep and goats, and everything. I was also working in the fields, hoeing and trying to help the crops to grow. I was also cooking and washing for everybody. And while I was working, I was wondering why Alexis was still cold. He would come home at the end of every month, but he was always not well. His kidneys bothered him. When he tried to lift a heavy thing, he would be in pain.

We need the money, so he had to go to work, all summer and autumn. But then comes another winter, 1965. In August he cannot move his legs from the cold. He went to hospital again, and I was two months pregnant. He told me he wanted to work, so he can help us with money, and he tried to work even when his legs were hurting. So he worked and he worked until one day he fell where he was standing. His legs would not hold him. There was nothing, he said. No feeling in them. It was like he had no legs at all. Nothing underneath him. A man working beside him tried to pick him up and asked, 'Why did you fall?'

Alexis said he didn't know.

So from that day he was not going to work again, ever. Those legs were not going anywhere. Men from his job brought him to the hospital, and at the hospital they started to treat him, and they sent me a message that he was there.

Again I took the small children to my mother and began to walk to Maseru every week to visit Alexis. I took my only daughter, Manraile, with me, and Mofihli on my back. Alexis was afraid I would lose the baby, so he said I should stay with the relatives in Lithabaneng, and not go back and forth to Roma. But when you stay with relatives, you have to buy food for the whole family and take food to the person who is sick. I was too poor; I could not buy all this food. So I would take one whole day, walking from Roma to Lithabaneng. I would sleep at Lithabaneng, and then walk half the day to Maseru. After visiting Alexis, I would walk back to Lithabaneng and sleep again; and the next day walk home to Roma.

I tried to find work, to earn some money while I was in Roma, but it was hard to find work because I was pregnant. Manraile was eight years old, and we were both very strong, so we fell into a kind of pattern of walking to Maseru every week, and soon it felt like it was our life to do this. We would take *motoho*, a sour porridge drink, in a canteen; and *papa* and *moroho* in a cake tin. Sometimes there would be water on the way; sometimes no water. Manraile had no shoes. I had some old shoes that were falling apart, but they still had a little bit of sole to protect my feet from the stones, so I was a little bit better off.

Alexis was in Ward Five again. His legs were very big and wrapped in cottonwool. He said, 'I can't see how I can ever use these legs again,' and he was very sad. 'What am I going to do for you and the children?'

They gave him a wheelchair, so he could move around in the hospital, but he could see that he was not ever going to leave that place. He could not move with a wheelchair in the mountains. He could not even go anywhere in Roma, or Maseru. There were not so many roads then, and no sidewalks. A wheelchair was useless except in the hospital.

So when it was almost time for the baby to come, I went back to the mountains. In February 1966, I got a baby boy, Muso. We named him Muso, which means Government, because he was born in the year of independence, and my father-in-law didn't have to pay tax to the British anymore. Before independence, every man, no matter how poor, had to pay tax to the British or he was put in jail. My father-in-law was glad not to pay tax anymore, so we named the baby Muso. But my heart was troubled because of Alexis. I stayed in the mountains for the harvest. 'M'anthabiseng came with me to help me have the baby, and she worked with me in the fields. It was a good year; we had plenty of sorghum and green split peas. We dried them and put them in big baskets.

Then I left Tseliso and Motlatsi in the mountains and I went back to Roma with Mofihli, Ralibuseng, Manraile, and with Muso on my back. I needed Manraile to help me with the little boys; there was no time for her to go to school. I was sorry for that. She never went to school until she was eleven, because I needed her help.

In Roma we stayed with my mother. My mother was living alone when I was in the mountains, and she was very happy to have us all with her. My mother always worried when we were in the mountains. She said she didn't like us to be there, because when we were hungry we were going to sleep with that hunger. It was half a day to the shop and half a day back, and no money to buy anything at the shop if we could get there.

As soon as we got back to Roma, I took only one day to rest and I went to the hospital to see Alexis. I took only Muso and Manraile with me. Muso was nursing, and Manraile went along to help carry the baby. When we arrived at the hospital, it was the first time for Alexis to see Muso. Alexis cried tears, and he told the nurses, 'Look at my child. He finds me in the hospital with nothing to wear. Now I have no money to help my children. I worked many, many years, and now my boy finds me this way.'

The nurses were afraid of Alexis because he was sometimes very angry. He would shout at them and say he wants to go out and work for his children. But he was too sick. His legs would not work. And when the nurses saw him crying and holding his baby boy, they could not stay in the room. They covered their faces and went out.

Again I fall into the pattern of walking to Maseru with Manraile. Muso on my back. There were very few cars in that time. Once a coal truck passed us, and the man driving the coal truck said, 'Look at this woman and these small children. I must give them a ride.'

So we got on top of the coal in the back of the truck. I hated that. It was windy and dirty there. It was my first time and I never did it again. We walked all the other times, until 1967. I go because it's right for me to go. If I didn't go, I would dream many bad dreams. It was hard, but I felt I must go. My mother felt the same thing. She was very sympathetic with Alexis. She was worried, because Alexis helped her many times. When we finished harvesting maize, he used to come with a donkey and give sacks of maize to my mother. When we slaughtered a sheep, he brought her the meat. He liked her very much, so she also felt I must go to hospital to see him. One day I told Alexis that I was going home to the Maluti because it was time to plough. He says, 'What are you going to do there for food, because I'm here? I don't want you to go back. I want you to stay here in Maseru and come to visit me.'

I say, 'What about your sheep and goats?' I was selling the sheep from the mountains. I would sell one or two at a time to get money for paraffin and maize meal. At that time you could get four rands for each sheep. One rand would be enough for a big bag of maize meal. But some of the sheep were stolen in the mountains.

When they started to steal, they took thirty sheep in one night. From there they took one animal every night. Tseliso, my oldest boy, was watching the animals by day, but the thieves took them at night. There was no one to stay up all the time and watch the animals, and we thought the thieves were many. No child alone could stop them. I didn't tell Alexis all of this, because he would worry too much, and there was nothing he could do.

He says, 'I told you to sell all the animals and bring the money to the bank, so you can help the children to go to school. Look at Manraile. She is going up and down with you because she has to carry the baby when you are tired. I don't like this. I want to get out of this hospital so I can help you.'

So one of the doctors said, 'Alexis, you must not go out of this hospital, because the government will no longer pay money for your treatment if you leave.' The doctor said that since Alexis was hurt while he was working for the government, the government pays money for him each month he is in hospital, money for the family and money to pay the cost of the hospital.

It was my first time to hear this. The doctor tells me a cousin of Alexis who speaks very good English gets the money for our family, and I am supposed to go to him for the money. This cousin works in Maseru and he goes to the government to get the money for us.

So I go to that cousin. He says, 'Oh, this is not a good time to come for the money. Come next month.'

I go the next month and he says, 'There is no money this month. Come again next month.'

Every month it is the same way. In time I quit going to him, but I know he is taking Alexis's money, the money for our family. My mother tells me not to worry, because this cousin is rich. She says rich people are always like this: greedy. But she says God will bring him down in the end, and we should say nothing to him.

I notice that this man built himself a very nice house while Alexis is in hospital. I know he is building with our money. When this man sees me, even now, he always has shame. I know he kept our money. So all the time Alexis was sick, I had no money. My mother was working in people's gardens, and she made enough money to buy a little maize meal, some paraffin and soap. We ate *papa*, *moroho* and peas from my fields. That is why I don't like peas now. I ate them too many years. I can't eat them anymore.

So I keep going to see Alexis in the hospital. His legs were in bandages. I want to see the wounds, but the nurses tell me I cannot look at his legs, or I can be sick. They say the meat comes off his bones. He was getting weaker and weaker, and very sick. One day he told the nurses, 'I know that wife of mine has no money to come see me, but please telephone to the police station in Roma; tell her to come and see me, and bring Muso, because I am very sick and I want to see them one more time.'

When the police find me and give me this message, I borrow money for the bus so I can go to Maseru quickly. I take Muso on my back. I find Alexis in a special room in the hospital alone, and he is very ill, in so much pain his face is gray and he is almost too weak to speak or move. He says to me, 'I'm sick, my wife, but I will help you all I can.' He was very glad to see Muso. He asks me to give him the child. I lay Muso on the bed beside him, and he uses all the strength he has, to take the child and hold him to his heart. He says, 'Oh, my child, you are going to be poor.'

I cannot stand to see him feel so much pain of heart. I try to give him some hope. I say, 'Why? Because you are going to be well, and come out of this hospital, and you will be able to work again.' I say that, but I know he is so sick, he can't be better. I think maybe I can take him home to die there. And as if he is reading my mind, he says, 'Yes. Tomorrow I want you to come with a *koloi* and take me home with you. I'm tired of this hospital. But be sure you come early, before nine o'clock.'

I tell him nine o'clock is too early. I can't go back to Roma, find a *koloi*, and bring someone back here with me that early, but he says, 'You must try, so that we can go home.'

Outside the room I find a nurse. I tell her I am going to Roma to try to find a person who has a *koloi*; to take Alexis home. She says no. She says Alexis is very sick; when they wash him, the meat goes away from his bones as if a dog has eaten him. We cannot move him from that bed. There is no going home for him now. She says I must prepare for his funeral.

I go back to Roma on the bus, and my heart is very sore. Alexis was in so much pain, and he was sick for such a long time, I think it can be better for him when he is dead. In my mind I see many times how he held Muso to his heart. I feel Muso move against my back, and I think about the nurse, telling me to prepare for the funeral. But I have no money to prepare.

At 10 o'clock the next day a policeman comes to my door. He says he got a phone call to say that Alexis passed away at 9 o'clock that morning. It was August 1968. Again I borrow money; again I go to Maseru. At the hospital they tell me, 'This person should not be taken home for burial. We know that you are alone; you have no one to help you. The government will help you to bury your husband here and will buy his coffin.'

So we buried him there, close to the hospital. You could not even call it a funeral. It was only me and his one brother and sister who lived in Lithabaneng. They had let me sleep at their house many times when I was coming to see Alexis. Now they came with me for his burial. We took him straight from the hospital to the cemetery. There was no feast, no nothing. After that, I went home again to Roma.

I planned to go to the Maluti the next day, to tell Alexis's father. But in the morning before I left, Alexis's father arrived. Every day Radio Lesotho announces all the deaths from that day, and *Ntate* heard from the radio that Alexis died. He was too late for the funeral, or rather the burial. So I walked back to the Maluti with *Ntate*. We slept on the way, as always, and we arrived at home just as the sun was setting. It was always Alexis's favourite time to be in the mountains, to sit in front of our little rondavel and watch the sunset.

In the morning our neighbours came. I cut my hair and took all my clothes off and put on my old clothes that I had left behind when I went to Roma. I did not have money for black clothes. We stayed in the mountains August, September and October. Then I came back to Roma again, with the last of the animals that had not been stolen: ten sheep, one cow, and one horse. I left all my things in the house as if I would be coming back. Left everything. Left the rondavel with a nice door. Just left it all there and went to work at the University, cleaning houses.

An Unexpected Daughter

'M'AMOROOSI 'M'ASEELE QACHA

She rose at the sound of a cock's crow. She could hear it much clearer now, and she smiled at her great achievement. She said to herself, 'Didn't they say I was stupid to travel to the next town to pick this cock? Now see how reliable it is. Not one of these weak ones that feed on *moroko*. The stuff gets them drunk and they can never wake one up early.'

The rays of the sun were just emerging between the high mountains, the mist still visible at their peaks. As she stood at the door, she watched the beautiful mountain scenery which she had over the years grown to love. These mountains were all she knew; she had never left that part of her beloved country, had never seen any other land and had no wish to do so. She was content with what she had. 'Thabang!' she shouted, 'Thabang, wake up, you lazy boy. Just as lazy as your uncle.' She thought, 'How can he be asleep until this late? Not with all the work that needs to be done.' Still standing in the doorway she added, 'Thabang, you had better wake up before I get there, or you are asking for it!'

She starts walking angrily towards the *mokhoro*, where Thabang and his two younger brothers sleep, thinking, 'Why did this man have to die and leave me with these lazy boys? The kraal is full of cattle and sheep, and all they can do is to sleep and not take care of them. How I miss Thabiso! Thabiso is an obedient boy and a hard worker, too.' Thabiso, her eldest son, is away at University.

She knocks at the door and opens it wide.

'Thabang, ha o utloe? Ke ntse ke u bitsa.' (Thabang, can't you hear? I'm calling you.) She walks right into the small dark room and looks around for Thabang, but before she can see him, she sees the shadow of a person behind the door.

'Who is behind the door?' she shouts out. 'Thabang, who is the person behind the door?' Thinking and acting quickly she grabs a stick nearby and charges at the figure. Thabang jumps up, grabs the stick, and attempts to stop his mother.

'*Ntsetse, Ntsetse, butle! Ha e ka o batla ho bolaea mosali oa ka tje?*' (Ntsetse, Ntsetse, hold it! Why do you want to kill my wife?) says Thabang in a big fright.

'M'athabiso stops dead in her tracks.

'What the hell are you talking about? What wife? Whose wife? Since when did you have a wife?'

'*Ntsetse*, we have to talk,' Thabang said, trying his best to be gentle. By this time his mother was not reacting too well to the shock.

'Talk? talk? what talk? Get this girl the hell out of my house.' With that she walked out. She could think of only one thing: how was she going to manage? Already she had more than enough mouths to feed, what with their father being killed by the mine shaft and all. She was having a tough enough time as it was, and now this. She would have to pay the parents of that girl for *chobeliso* and then *likhomo tsa ho nyala*. No. She made up her mind. The girl would have to go home.

'M'athabiso had a job some fifty miles away; it was enough to pay school fees for the boys in the local primary school and to buy them a few trousers. How could she possibly afford to feed and clothe another child? What with this stupid young man going out and dragging that poor girl – she wondered how old the girl must be. Hardly fifteen years, she supposed. What about this stupid boy, only sixteen years. 'The stupid fool,' she thought, 'can't even wait to finish high school. He is already chasing after girls. If only he could have been patient, he would have finished high school in three years; then he would be free to do as he wished. Now look at this mess I'm in as a consequence of all this.'

As all these thoughts revolved in her head, the sun was slowly rising, the fog on the mountains lifting and disappearing. She felt alone, lost. The world seemed larger, wider, and she felt ever smaller. She saw nothing, heard nothing, and felt nothing, only the thoughts, too many to be sorted out, to make sense of, or to be put into comprehensible sequence. Somewhere there had to be a solution. She would go to her husband's brother, now the person she was responsible to – her 'father'.

'He is a wise man,' she thought. 'He has handled this sort of thing many times before and will know what is to be done.' The thought of help gave her inspiration and energy she didn't know she had in her. She ran the full mile uphill to her brother-in-law's house. She arrived there breathless. As she knocked on the door she walked in. Her brother-in-law was sitting at the kitchen table having his breakfast. As the door burst open, he looked at the doorway. He saw the vision of a woman, dressed in a skimpy dress, shawl around her waist, and no shoes on her feet. He could see that it was 'M'athabiso, the wife to his own brother. But something about her seemed to be different. He couldn't tell what it was, but something seemed to be wrong with her.

'Yes,' he thought, 'she does not normally come here this early. And definitely, she's always well-dressed and smart looking.' What he saw was not normal, and with that he rose to his feet to welcome her inside.

She walked in slowly, unsure of what to say next. She sat down, greeted in a low voice. Her brother-in-law replied, still standing, ''M'athabiso, what is the problem?'

She could not help sobbing as she related the events of the early morning: 'I don't know what to do. This child has defeated me. I have no strength to go on.' Slowly, she related what had happened.

As she spoke, her brother-in-law was still on his feet. Now he sat down and looked her straight in the face, saying, ''M'athabiso, today you are a mother-in-law. You have a daughter-in-law. You know as much as I do that there is no way the girl can return to her home, *o shobetse* (she has eloped), and so she is now your daughter and the wife of your son. There is no undoing that. Today God has given you the daughter that you have always wanted and prayed for. As you know, *Molimo ha a fe motho ka letsoho*, God never gives anyone with his hand. From today the daughter you now have will help you, not only with the household chores but also in the fields. Now, instead of two hands, you have four.'

'M'athabiso listened, and as she listened a warmth of hope

surged through her. She had never thought of it this way. The only things she had considered were the extra problems and costs she would incur as a result of this girl. Now, as she listened, she saw the other side of the coin and she thought, 'I was right. This was the man to come to.'

But something still worried her, so she told her brother-in-law, 'Yes, I agree, I have always wanted a daughter who could help me, but not this way. I want my son to get education. I don't want him to be like us, wholly dependent on this poor farming. If he is to marry now, there is no way he can continue with his schooling. He will now have to go and look for work in order to feed his wife and to clothe her. You know yourself how poor the crops have been lately. There is no way these children can survive if one of them does not work. I say the girl must go back to her home. What about her? She is too young to leave her family. She has no idea what marriage is all about. How can you expect her to take care of a husband and in a few years, children? Imagine, a fifteen-year-old child having another child. She is only a baby herself. No. It is impossible. It's out of the question.'

'That's why it is a blessing,' the brother-in-law, Ramaise, said. 'Like your own daughter, you will grow her. You will teach her everything that she needs to know, and in her will emerge a loving, intelligent, honest, hard-working woman, just like you.'

M'athabiso did not reply. She was quiet for a long time, as she put together all the thoughts, trying hard to reconcile the bitter-sweet facts that faced her. The girl could not go back. It was traditional. Nothing like that was ever done. At the same time, none of 'M'athabiso's plans included the girl. She had thought she had it all figured out: the boys would all go to university to become teachers, doctors, or lawyers. Now it meant a complete rescheduling of plans. She tried to fit the girl in to her view of things. Would she go to school? Would she remain at home the whole day? Would she become a nurse, a teacher, or . . . ? Oh, this was driving her out of her mind.

'Now, what do we do?' she finally asked.

''M'athabiso,' Ramaise said to her, 'Thabang has made a decision in his life, to become a husband and father, to start his own family. All these things you are worried about will be decided and solved by Thabang, as the head of his family, and of course with advice from you. So I am advising you, don't worry too much about this. Things will work themselves out. From here, we have to inform and invite the girl's family to the wedding ceremony. In the meantime we make arrangements for the wedding and build a new *mokhoro* for the newlyweds. By wedding I don't mean much. All we need to do is to slaughter one of the sheep, so that the girl can be traditionally welcomed. We will have to buy her a dress, a blanket, and a pair of shoes for the occasion, and that is all.'

'M'athabiso felt a relief that she had never thought possible. She felt like she had been unloaded of a ton of bricks. 'You mean that is all?'

After she said that, she remembered that 'M'amotsoari's son got married in the exact same manner, only two months ago. Now that she could think clearer, she remembered that there was not much that happened there. She felt herself smiling and couldn't believe how quickly her misery had disappeared. Yes, that was it. The girl would be customarily welcomed to the family, after which Thabang would have to make decisions and plans for his family. She thought, 'If he will have to go to the mines for employment, so be it. He has to support his family. A man has to do what a man has to do.'

Ramaise told 'M'athabiso to go back home. He said he would tell his wife about the matter, after which he would inform members of the family and dispatch some of them to the girl's family to pass the message.

'M'athabiso walked out, much slower. The sun was shining brightly by now. She could tell from the rise of the sun that it was around 8 o'clock, at which time she ought to have been at work. Her brain told her that she ought to hurry home, get washed and go to work, but her body refused her. She felt tired and drained of all energy. She walked home slowly, the stones on the road stinging the soles of her bare feet. As she walked, she wondered what had urged Thabang to marriage.

'Maybe,' she thought, 'it's the influence of his friends. Most of those boys have gone and married very young girls, and instead of being men, they have become burdens to their families. Anyway, we shall see.'

She arrived home, washed herself, and dressed. Then, she called Thabang and told him of their plans to hold a small wedding for them. Now, she wanted to know his plans for the future. So he told her that he wanted to complete his schooling, but he had to fetch this girl because they had been together until late, and the girl had refused to go back to her home, claiming that she had been scared to go. That had left him with little choice but to bring her here. He supposed that she would also go to school, as she had expressed the need to complete her schooling. He said he was aware of financial problems that prevailed, but he promised that they would work hard to help their mother with the field and garden, to provide for food. During the holidays they would have to get employment in town to complement their mother's small salary, so as to ensure that school fees were paid. In the unfortunate event of these plans not coming to life, the girl would have to leave school, so that he could get the necessary education to find good employment. Thereafter he would sponsor her schooling.

'M'athabiso felt extreme pride as she listened. Overnight, her son had turned into a man, able to consider all possibilities open to him, able to assess the situation and find his way out of it. She looked at him, thinking,' How young he looks. So innocent and inexperienced, and yet he could come up with all this.' She found herself speechless as she continued to look at him. At last she said to him, 'Being a man is not easy. You will have to work hard, and when I say hard, I mean that from today I don't have to wake you up again. When I wake up I expect to find the animals out of the kraal, the chickens fed, and you ready to go to school. Lastly, you have to pass well at school to ensure that you get in to university. I hope I have made myself clear. I am prepared to do my part, if you do yours.'

So it was. The day of the wedding arrived. The sun rose much as on other days; the cock's crow sounded much the same and was just as punctual. The mist capped the peaks of the mountains as usual. Only the emotions and anxieties of 'M'athabiso and her family were different that day. For them, excitement was in the air. Some home-brewed beer had been prepared the previous night as well as some other food; one of the cattle had been slaughtered and some supplies purchased in town. As the big day began, the main item on the agenda was to cook the food and to get ready for the feast, so that by the time the girl's family arrived, everything would be just right.

As it turned out, the feast was ample and everyone had a great time, with a lot of singing and drinking. The girl was named 'M'aliteboho, a great lady of the clan. As the busy day came to an end, 'M'athabiso found herself looking toward the mountain range. The sun had set and all that was visible were the last glowing fiery rays. Most of the guests had gone, but a few relatives were finishing off the cleaning. It was very quiet, compared to a few hours earlier, and by now she could feel the fatigue in her bones.

'Well, at least that chapter is done,' she thought. 'Time to move on to the next.' She felt the need to rest a bit. As she walked towards the house she heard herself pray, 'Please, God, no more surprises. No more.' With that, she closed the door to her small house, took off her shoes and threw herself on her bed. For the first time in the last week she felt a deep sense of relief and dozed off.

The Lost Sheep is Found

TEMBELA SELEKE

'At last God Almighty has given me a friend who is courageous enough to make my dreams come true,' thought Usiwe to herself.

Usiwe had left her home in the Transkei on the ninth day of December 1981. She did not leave Umtata only; she also left her two kids behind, with her mother. She left all that was hers, taking only four dresses with her when she left for Lesotho, because she was expecting to spend only two weeks away from home. She had forgotten the Xhosa proverb which says, *Ungabali amantsontso inkuku ingekaqanduseli.* (Never count the chickens before they are hatched.) Usiwe had only gone to Lesotho to pay her husband Ben, who had been in Lesotho for the past five months, a visit. On Usiwe's arrival in Maseru, Ben said, *'Mna andinamfazi uza kuhlala kude nam.'* (I don't have a wife who can stay far from me.) Usiwe had to choose between staying with Ben and going back home to the children. She stayed. A year later Ben was among those refugees who were assassinated by the South African Defence Force during the 1982 December massacre in Lesotho. Usiwe had to remain in Lesotho after Ben's death because she was then a suspect in South Africa.

During her stay in Maseru, Usiwe found work. It was at this job that she met a colleague, Neo, who became her closest friend. In their conversations, Usiwe confided to Neo the reasons that brought her to Lesotho and added that there was no way of going back because *E ne e se e le leshala MaBurung.* (She was a suspect of the Boers.) Neo did not understand why Usiwe was afraid to go back, since Usiwe had not been involved in political activity. So Neo decided to make Usiwe cross the border and see that there was no danger.

One day, Neo told Usiwe that she was going to Ladybrand, the

South African border town outside Maseru, for shopping on Tree Planting Day.* Neo mentioned it lightly to Usiwe a week in advance. Usiwe timidly considered the possibility.

'*Ke tsamae le uena?*' (Can I go with you?)

'*E e.*' (Yes.)

'*Na o tiile?*' (Are you serious?)

'*E e.*' (Yes.)

Usiwe was not sure whether Neo was serious. A day before the Tree Planting Day, as her tension increased, Usiwe reminded Neo that she had promised they would go together. Neo had still not changed her mind.

'Where do we meet, then?'

'Let's meet next to the Post Office,' replied Neo.

'At what time?'

'At 10:00 a.m.'

'OK, see you tomorrow then. *Feela e seke eaba o ntse o bapala ka 'na?*' (Are you not making a fool of me?)

'*Ke tiile. Ha ke soasoe. Ha ree hosane.*' (I am serious. I'm not joking. Let's go tomorrow.)

When Usiwe got home from Roma, where she was attending university, she informed Khabele, her husband of five years, of the plan. Khabele voiced no objection. Tree Planting Day arrived. Usiwe reminded Khabele that she was going to Ladybrand. Usiwe was afraid, but she tightened herself. She was cross at Khabele when he said, '*A tla ho tsoaro MaBuru.*' (The Boers will arrest you.)

'Why did you agree last week when I first told you this?'

'I thought you were joking.'

'For how long will I stay in this country without knowing whether I can cross the borders or not? I am tired of saying I am afraid of the Boers, and yet I don't know what is it that I fear. Above that, I want to know if I will ever go home or not so that if not, I can forget about going home for the rest of my life.'

'*O! Ho lokile; he tsamaea.*' (Oh! OK, you can go.) Khabele was afraid that the Boers were going to arrest his sweetheart. However, he gave up. Before he left for work the following day he

---

* A public holiday observed on 23 March each year.

said, '*Le tsamae hantle he le khutle.*' (Have a pleasant journey and come back.)

'*Re tla tsamaea hantle.*' (We'll have a good journey.)

Usiwe woke up at 7:00 a.m. Anxiety did not allow her to sleep more. She was ready to go by 8:45 a.m. She left for the Post Office, thinking she would rather be early for the appointment than late. Usiwe was at the Post Office by 9:30 a.m. She waited for Neo patiently. Neo arrived at 10:10. Usiwe did not even wait for Neo to greet.

'*Ke ne ke nahana hore ose o inyatsitse,*' (I thought you had changed your mind,) Usiwe said.

'*Khale o le teng?*' (Have you been here long?)

'*Ke fihlile ka* half past nine.'

'*Ha re e he.*' (Let's go then.)

The two took a taxi to the border gate. Neo did not expect any trouble from the Boers. On the other hand, Usiwe did not expect a smooth journey. Usiwe was expecting something either on the way to or from Ladybrand. Usiwe did not want to talk about her expectations in case she might frighten Neo. In the taxi, the two women talked about general issues which were not at all associated with their journey.

At the border gate, on the South African side, there were long queues of people who were going to the Republic for various reasons. One immigration officer appeared and announced, 'Shopping. Shopping. Shopping.'

Usiwe's stomach was aching at the bottom. Her hand was even shaking *ngathi uphethwe lidumbe* (like someone who has a shivering sickness) when she was filling in the forms. They completed the forms. They passed their passports to the officer who was asking for passports from those who were going for shopping.

The officer collected a handful of passports and disappeared into one of the offices with them. Usiwe was standing next to the window. She wanted to see everything that was done with her passport. Usiwe saw two passports being checked against the list of the 'wanted'. During that process, Usiwe's heart beat so fast and so loudly that she thought the person next to her was hearing it. The minutes that the officer took to process the passports appeared to her as hours. She perspired under the feet like a dog. She tightened her dry mouth as if to prevent her *letsoalo* from escaping. Usiwe thought that the passports would be returned to their owners immediately after they were checked. In that way, Usiwe could see whether hers was among the doubtful ones. However, the officer was clever. After checking the passports, he returned with them to the office. When returning them, he shuffled the whole handful together.

Neo was standing at a distance of two metres. She had already received her passport and was waiting for Usiwe. Usiwe got hers back, too. No questions, nothing.

On receiving her passport, Usiwe smeared her dry lips and even got some drink to recall her saliva. Her bladder suddenly felt full; going to the toilet was a great relief. Then the two women entered the Republic of South Africa. Usiwe's heart jumped with joy on the one hand, while her stomach ached at the bottom on the other.

'I told you,' said Neo.

'No. I don't believe all this. No questions. Nothing. No man, this can't be true.'

'There is nothing that is going to happen.' Neo didn't know enough to understand Usiwe's fear.

'Well, we'll see.'

Usiwe did not want to say it was over. She would wait to say that when she entered Lesotho again. Neo didn't know that the Boers were awaiting her friend in Ladybrand. The two women took another taxi to their destination. They got off at the taxi rank. The time was 11:00 a.m. sharp.

Neo was going to pay her accounts. After making payments, the two women went to the OK Bazaars for shopping. After that, Usiwe wanted to go to Russells. But unfortunately, when they got to Russells, the shop was closed for lunch hour. The two women could not come to any agreement as to whether they should wait till 2:00 p.m. or go home. When they got to the taxi rank, Usiwe said that she was hungry. Neo showed her a café just opposite the taxi rank. They crossed the street. At the entrance to the cafe, Neo decided to remain outside with the parcels they were carrying so that Usiwe could go into the café to buy some food.

While Usiwe was bending to put her plastic bags beside Neo's, she saw a white hand appear from her left side. This hand held something in front of Usiwe's eyes. Usiwe was unable to read what was in the hand, because she was in a state of shock. Usiwe followed the hand while still bent over. She saw an arm like a *thithiboea*. Hairy all over. That was enough for her to know something had gone wrong.

'Accompany me to the office. Are you going with her?' he asked Neo. Back to Usiwe: 'Do you have a passport with you? *Kom. Kom. Maak gou.*' (Come. Come. Hurry up.) All these words were spoken in a harsh voice. The questions were asked one after another without even a pause for an answer. Poor Neo. She was still not aware of what was happening. Neo thought that maybe the Boers suspected some theft. Usiwe knew what was happening, but there was no way she could inform Neo now. There were two Afrikaner Special Branch (SB) policemen leading the way to their office. Behind Neo and Usiwe, there was another SB, black in this case. These SBs were sure that they had trapped their target, Usiwe.

The two women had been followed by the SBs, at a distance, from 11:00 a.m. until the time when the SBs thought they were going back to Lesotho. At that point the SBs decided to show themselves.

When the two women got to the office, which has its entrance locked with iron bars, they were taken to one room. The police gave them seats. Usiwe did not look these SBs in the eyes; she looked down. Usiwe could tell from the movement of the feet she saw that many people were coming in to see the 'wanted' woman. Neo was still blank. The SB who had shown his identity document at the café entrance took Usiwe's handbag, emptied it on the table, took her passport, opened it and said, 'No, this is a lie. This is a lie. Where is your other passport?'

'I don't have another.'

'What have you been using all these years?'

'I was not crossing the borders.'

'Why?'

'Because I was afraid.'

'Afraid of what?'

'I don't know.'

This SB opened each and every piece of paper that was in Usiwe's handbag but found nothing of importance. Usiwe was still looking down, when she saw the door opening at an angle of forty-five degrees. Nobody entered the room. Her sixth sense could tell her that there was somebody standing at the door. Usiwe lifted her eyes.

She got the shock of her life. Usiwe felt as if chilled water was poured down her spine. Tears filled her eyes at the sight of Suzan peeping out through the door. Suzan looked at Usiwe, to the SB, back at Usiwe, and, at last, she nodded in approval. Usiwe was watching her.

It was at the nod of Suzan that it occurred to Neo, who was also watching Suzan, that this was something different from what she had assumed. The SB who seemed to be the senior official ordered that Neo be taken to another office. But it was late.

'*Molo sis 'Maradebe*,' (Good afternoon, my sister) Suzan said, as she had long ago called Usiwe at the camp.

'*Ewe*.' (Yes.)

Suzan was confirming to the SB that the person in front of them was the right person. One of the Afrikaner SBs ordered another SB to bring Usiwe's file. This was a surprise to Usiwe; she didn't know that she had a file there. Usiwe was questioned, and the answers she gave were matched to the information in the file. But this Afrikaner wanted to force Usiwe to admit that she had been trained as a revolutionary in that camp with Suzan eight years before. Usiwe used Suzan as her witness.

'Ask Suzan. I never trained. I was there with Ben, but I was never politically active.' Usiwe was at Suzan's mercy. Luckily, Suzan came to Usiwe's rescue and denied all that Usiwe had denied.

'Oh! She is telling the truth. She never trained.'

The Afrikaner went through the file to satisfy himself. At long last he said to the other SB officials who were in the room, 'She is telling the truth.' This Afrikaner was down-spirited because of his disappointment. He made some general conversation with Usiwe after satisfying himself that she was not a threat to them. 'Then you have no problem with South Africa, but we do not know about the Transkei.'

This pleased Usiwe so much that she would have wagged her tail if she had one, but of course she had none. Usiwe did not fear anything from the Transkeian police; her problem was the stubborn 'pinkies' (Boers).

After rescuing Usiwe, Suzan left for the room where Neo was. Neo asked Suzan how things were going in there. Suzan couldn't answer because of her embarrassment. Suzan, having been at the training camp with Ben and Usiwe, had since been enticed by the police to become an informer. Usiwe had been Suzan's best friend, and Suzan was ashamed for Usiwe to see what she was doing now.

Neo emphatically told Suzan and the other police that she was not leaving Usiwe behind. Neo added that if they detained Usiwe, they should prepare enough room for both of them. It was about 3:30 p.m. when Usiwe was dismissed.

Usiwe was no longer interested in going to Russells. She and Neo rushed for the taxi after refusing an offer to be taken to the border gate by a black SB. They feared they might be called back to that tense office again.

It was a joy when Usiwe got home and told Khabele about that day's achievement. When Khabele had come back from work that evening, he had been afraid to ask the children where their mother was, for fear they might say she was not back yet.

In December the same year, Usiwe phoned home and made arrangements for her younger brother to come and collect her immediately after her mid-term examinations. Her parents could not believe their ears. However, Usiwe's younger brother came, and they left for the Transkei on 23 December 1990. For the first time in a full nine years, Usiwe set her foot home. Two days later, the relatives were called to rejoice at the reappearance of the sheep which had long been lost. Those who managed to come could not believe their eyes.

Give Me a Chance

MZAMANE NHLAPO

Mama KaZili woke up early with her eyes red and watery as though she had been crying the whole night. I suspected that something was going to happen. At the age of nine I could see and observe well. Life at home demanded as much.

That was the day when she decided never to let us die of hunger. My father had not been sending her money from the South African mines for more than a year. It was said that he had another wife in the mines. His parents refused to listen to Mama KaZili's complaints about that. They wanted her to accept that for a husband to have numerous wives was a norm, something a 'good' wife did not have to complain about. They did not seem to understand the economic realities facing her and her children.

But in a way it was understandable why my grandparents didn't care. If my father sent money at all, he sent it to his mother, who was to decide whether to pass it on to Mama KaZili. So in most cases Mama KaZili never received a cent. My father knew this, but he too could not afford a complaining wife.

'Today we are going to Makhoakoeng, to some relatives of your father,' my mother announced that morning after we had eaten *papa mplothe*.

'Why, mother?' I asked. She took time to answer my question. I saw her swallow something hard first.

'Because if we stay here you won't have something to eat,' she said eventually.

Makhoakhoeng is forty kilometres from Habelo, my home village. To go there we took an old bus from Botha-Bothe, my home town. After travelling for thirty kilometres, there was no road for the bus to go further. The Maluti Mountains began to get rough. Steep, rocky, real rough. Worse still, it was snowing that day. The air was chilly and freezing to the bone-marrow, more so when we were wrapped in tattered blankets and had no shoes on our feet. A sympathetic woman must have lent my mother some money at home so that we could take the bus to those mountains. They were so white and so huge, those mountains!

Slowly we began to climb those cold, slippery and uncompromising mountains. My younger sister, Nopaseka, fell down time and again, each time getting herself more damp from the snow. At one time I decided to carry her on my back because my mother had the youngest baby, Mkhathini, on hers. Nopaseka was too heavy for me, and we fell down together. My mother also fell, only twice or thrice. Mothers are tough; they don't fall easily. But the last time she fell, it was real heavy, and I heard her mention my father's name in disgust: 'Moshe!' She also mentioned the names of my elder brother and sister who were left at home, as if to say, 'What will they do tonight?' When I walked close enough to her, her eyes were still a little red and looked like they had water in them.

We struggled up the mountains in a numbing temperature. I could not feel my toes. Our faces were stung by the chilling winter winds. A vicious icy snow pelted us in the face. Our bodies were bruised, hungry and exhausted. But we were determined to reach the place of our father's relatives where we would eat *papa* before we went to sleep. The determination of Mama KaZili rekindled ours.

We wrestled endlessly with the treacherous mountains to cover the ten kilometres. I could not calculate the passage of time. My mother kept swallowing something hard. She also spoke alone, uttering words like, 'I'll go back to work hard for them . . . Tonight you will eat . . .'

When we were close to the village we were going to, we stopped. Mama KaZili wanted to breastfeed the baby. The baby did not suck her breasts as usual. He was very stiff and looked very pale. And he was not breathing. For the first time in my life, I heard my mother cry.

The death of Mkhathini reduced our number to six in the home.

It is difficult to tell in detail exactly what went on in that snowy weather. But I do remember that we were taken to the village on horseback. Observant villagers had seen that we had stopped at one spot for a long time in the snow, and they must have wondered why. Then horsemen came to fetch us. People in the mountains are more concerned about others than people in the lowlands or towns.

When we arrived at my father's relatives, there was a mixture of happiness and grief. They were happy to see us: children of their brother. But the sight of Mama KaZili carrying the dead child was a great shock.

They might have been shocked and struck by the sight of death, but by this time Mama KaZili was sober, clear and determined. She was in her best poised manner. She was no longer a cold, crying woman trapped in the snow with small kids falling down numerous times behind her. I saw a mixture of anger, grit and will-power in her. That was my mother at her best.

She was expecting the accusation: 'If you respected your husband and his parents the child wouldn't have died.'

She knew that they, too, would be more concerned about the cultural norms and respect for the Nhlapo family than the circumstances that compelled her to come to them. One step wrong, she knew, and she would be told she was not married from Swaziland to kill children, but to 'make' them for the family to grow.

After the initial shock of Mkhathini's death was absorbed, and initial discussions about burying him had finished, Mama KaZili had to answer a few questions just as she had expected. The house was full of curious relatives, each one of them listening very attentively. The atmosphere was like in a serious village court case.

'You mean you didn't ask permission to come here from your husband or from my parents?' Matweba, my father's eldest brother, asked with serenity.

'Yes, after all I know they would have refused,' answered Mama KaZili coolly.

'And what lesson do you think you are teaching other wives in this big Nhlapo family?'

Mama KaZili kept silent.

'Talk!' scolded Matweba. Other men's voices joined his, uttering something like, 'Yeah, she must talk.'

'Talk!' repeated Matweba, shouting at the top of his voice.

Mama KaZili looked at him straight in the eye and said, 'I'm teaching them that when husbands don't fulfil their duties as heads and breadwinners of families, to an extent that children die of hunger, they should not sit there and do nothing, waiting for manna from heaven. I have brought my children to you for a month or two to have something to eat while I look for employment.'

'And again without permission?'

'Yes,' Mama KaZili answered with firmness.

There were some men's rumbling voices once again, this time louder and more threatening. I remembered one case two years ago back in Habelo when one woman had told her husband outright that he was lazy. Every corner of the village had groups of men cursing 'What an insult! A woman tell her husband he is lazy!' By the end of the week the woman had disappeared. Her husband had beaten her severely. Nobody knew exactly whether she had been admitted at the hospital, or had run back to her parents, *a ngalile*, or had joined other runaway wives who were eventually called prostitutes. The incident was surrounded by rumours and speculations until a few days later when dogs dug up the decaying body of the woman in her garden.

'Order!' Matweba demanded silence.

In addition to the rumblings, there was an uncomfortable chaotic movement in the house. Men felt insulted by Mama KaZili, and obviously some of them wanted to 'touch' or 'lay hands' on her. Others gaped at her with utter scorn.

'She must go back to Swaziland!' a voice shot to the roof.

'O-o-o-o-order!' Matweba shouted vehemently in a roar that could have frightened a lion.

There was a smell of onion from the other room. My stomach groaned. My mouth watered. If only we would eat in a few minutes! At least by now we were warm from yellowish-blue flames of burning dung. But we were still starving. Would we ever eat, amidst these heated quarrels of grown-ups? I wondered.

A group of birds passed next to the window singing their old melodious song happily as though it was not snowing outside. In the house a deafening silence fell once more for Mama KaZili to speak.

'May I remind you that I'm a legal citizen of Lesotho through marriage? I don't intend to go back to Swaziland. And no one can force me to go, not even my husband.'

'Does this woman ever read the Bible? Will she ever learn to respect us?' one man asked loudly near the door. Other voices joined in unison, 'Yes, the Bible. And respect us?' The question was directed to Mama KaZili via Matweba.

'Yes, I know the Bible,' she answered. 'It says women should keep silent: "they are commanded to be under obedience, as also saith the law."'* Customary laws also treat women as children who are supposed to be under the man's guidance and protection. Women are considered weak and naïve. They have to seek permission even for little things like visiting friends and parents; in looking for employment; when they want to go to school, or ask for a scholarship or a loan; in applying for a site . . . Name them all.' Mama KaZili told them in a clear, firm voice; her voice had a ring to it, like a medium-sized school bell. It indicated self-confidence, industriousness, fairness and humbleness, just a touch of hunger, loneliness and tiredness. The way everybody listened quietly in the house you would have thought they were hypnotised. Mama KaZili continued undisturbed.

'All these forms of gender inequalities and injustices take place in a government† that repeatedly points out with pride that it has been elected by women because men, who are predominantly away in the South African mines, are mostly pro-BCP.‡ Society and government don't want to give women a chance. Women have to seek permission for everything that can improve their lives. Before I pass away in this world I want to have had a chance to improve my life and the lives of my children.'

Everybody in the house was looking at her in disbelief,

---

* 1 Corinthians 14:34–35
† Basutoland National Party.
‡ Basutoland Congress Party.

open-mouthed and eyebrows raised. Mama KaZili must have given them more than enough to chew at a go. Men sighed without a word. One after the other they started going out of the house silently. The last to go was Matweba, who said in a declarative tone, 'Men solve family problems best at the kraal. We shall be back soon to give our final word on the matter.' He closed the door behind him with what I thought was a bang.

Fortunately for them, it had stopped snowing, although it was still freezing outside.

I heard a cow moo at the kraal, obviously mistaking the men for herdboys. Perhaps a communication of some kind to say, 'I did not eat enough grass during the day.'

As soon as the men had gone out, plates of food were brought in for us to eat. That was what Mama KaZili had brought us to Makhoakheng for: to have something to eat before we went to sleep. The food was delicious: *papa, papasane*, and mutton. It was two years since I had eaten meat. The smell of onion was there.

I had always been told that my nickname, 'Richman' was derived from one old Nhlapo whom I was named after, who lived at Makhoakhoeng sometime in the late 1890s, owning a lot of sheep. That day, with mutton in my plate, the nickname made a lot of sense.

There were mixed feelings about what Mama KaZili had said to the men. Elderly wives thought she shouldn't have spoken like that to the heads of families, and that she should offer an apology when they came back from the kraal. Younger wives thought the truth had finally been told. It was high time they stood up on their feet to do something about their lives, they said. Even if men did not admit it, economic pressures in the families appeared too heavy for them to lift alone. It was time they swallowed their pride and accepted reality. Mama KaZili nodded her head with satisfaction, agreeing with the younger women. Her preaching was developing roots.

One by one, in single file, the men came in. They were silent and frightening. Dusk made them look like tall black shades moving in silhouette. One by one they occupied their seats. Their sitting on chairs, while the women sat flatly on the floor, added

authority to the men. Once again, Matweba took the chairman-
ship.

Soon there was a frightening silence in the house. Those who
hadn't finished eating had to stop abruptly. The atmosphere
became charged like a live electric wire. Everybody knew that
decisions made from the kraal could not be questioned. In a way
the decisions were regarded as holy because men were made
heads of families by the Almighty God.

The last man came in from the other house, carrying a bundle
in his hands, wrapped in a white sheet. He put the bundle next to
my mother. It was the corpse of Mkhathini, the deceased child.
The audience remained breathless.

With a thundering note of finality in his voice, Matweba broke
the silence: 'I, Matweba, the brother of your husband, together
with his other close relatives, have decided that you, Mama
KaZili, are bringing disrespectful and misleading lessons to our
wives here at Makhoakhoeng. If they allow you to do that at
Habelo, we cannot allow it here. We have therefore decided that,
because of snow, the children will remain here for a week or so.
As soon as the snow is over they will be sent back to Habelo, back
to you. We cannot allow you to humiliate Moshe, your husband,
our brother, by scattering his children all around in the name of
looking for employment without anybody's permission. If we can
allow you to humiliate him, our wives can also get out of hand
and humiliate us. We cannot allow the disintegration of the
Nhlapo family. Those of us who have not been fortunate enough
to get employment in the mines have the duty of keeping the
Nhlapo family intact.

'Tomorrow morning some of us will accompany you back to
Habelo to help with the burial service for the deceased. You will
have to carry the corpse back home on your back, just like you
brought it here today. I have spoken.'

Indeed Matweba had spoken. As soon as he had finished,
everyone stood up to disperse to their families in silence. The
decision from the kraal had sounded very definite.

Matweba and his men might have been keeping culture,
customs and the Nhlapo family intact, but they were still in for
another surprise, another challenge. The decision from the kraal

was not definite and final enough for Mama KaZili. She stood up
to speak. Members of the family who were already going had to
stop to listen.

'You may have spoken. But I also have meant every word I
spoke to you and to everybody. It is up to us women to stand up
for our lives and the lives of our children . . . I'll go back to work
hard, hard for them and for myself . . .' She spoke aloud in a tone
that changed to a familiar one I had heard several hours ago
when we were struggling to climb the slippery, snowy mountain.

She did not finish all she wanted to say because she fell down
heavily, just like the last time she did on the mountain with a
baby on her back. But this time she did not utter the name of my
father in disgust when she fell. It was just a heavy and very
silent fall. Her body lay painfully crooked next to the body of
Mkhathini.

My sister and I were the first to cry hysterically. We did not
like the thought that our mother might have died too, leaving us
alone in the brutal, uncaring world.

Very quickly we were taken to the other house because we
were making unbearable noise and disturbing the adults. They
were pouring cold water on Mama KaZili's head to wake her up.

I recalled all the events of the day and all that Mama KaZili
had said. In one instance, she had said: 'Before I pass away in
this world I want to have had a chance to improve my life and the
lives of my children.' I wondered if this would ever materialise.

By the end of the year she would be working as a primary
teacher without my father's or his parents' permission. From her
meagre salary she sent us to school; again, without anybody's
permission. Since then, there was always something to eat before
we went to sleep.

Arriving Home in a Helicopter

JULIA 'M'AMATSELISO KHABANE

Translated by SR. ALINA KHABANE

I was sixteen years old when I left home in Matsoku, Ha Meno, to go to school in Maseru. I had never before left my home for Lesotho, as we used to call the lowlands. The only vehicle I had ever seen (but never boarded), was a big truck that used to bring maize meal and other goods to the store in our vicinity.

Let me take you back to those days.

The Standard Seven results were out and I had passed. Since I had lost both parents, the hope of furthering my studies had died. I was working as my brother's shepherd so that his son could go to school when the schools opened. But one day I got a letter from my sister in Maseru, and this letter revived my hopes.

> Marebetsana,
>
> You pleased me so much that I can run mad. I went to the examinations council offices to check your performance and found that you have obtained a second class. Since our mother, on her death-bed, told us to take good care of you, I have asked Ntate Thaane to allow you to come and stay with me so that you can attend school at Mabathoana High School.
>
> Please do not disappoint me, child of my mother, because you are an orphan of orphans. With this I want to give you a weapon to fight life. Come at your earliest convenience so that we can make all the necessary arrangements.
>
> Greet everybody at home.
>
> Your loving sister, 'M'alisebo.

I pinched myself. 'Am I awake or am I dreaming?' I had no way to get reassurance. '*Ag!* if this is a dream, what an accursed person will I be when I learn the truth!' With shaking hands, I brought the letter to *Ntate* Thaane, my brother-guardian. I was afraid of his response, so I sneaked out like a cat but did not go far, because I was eager to hear his reaction. Thinking that I was still standing by his side, he started talking, still perusing the letter.

'In Maseru, people do not walk with feet, so, the first thing we should do tomorrow is to go to the store and buy you shoes.'

He expected my reply in vain. Instead I was outside, dancing my joy out.

'This will be the first time I put a shoe on my foot,' I thought.

'Marebetsana! Are you mad?' roared my brother.

'*Potlololo!*' I became small like *theepe*, a wild vegetable, that has been brought to a boil.

'*E Ntate*,' I replied with a thin spirit.

'Why is your spirit so thin? Are you not happy about my sister's offer?' he bullied. 'Teboho!' shouted my brother to one of his sons.

'*Ntate*,' replied Teboho.

'Can you go to the fold and get one of those black and white sheep to make provision for your aunt?'

'*O! Ntate.*' Teboho was curious to know where I was going, but he could not ask in front of his father, so he ran to the kraal and brought a sheep.

'Why have you taken such a small one? Who knows? It may be it is the last time I do something for my sister. Let me go and show you the one I like.'

Orders were going from one direction to the other.

''M'akutloano, my wife, can you sort Marebetsana's clothes? Do not worry about blankets. 'M'alisebo will take care of that.'

Everybody was moving up and down for *ngoanan'a moroetsana* was going. The heart of the girl who was the source of all this commotion sang an endless song: '*Ku! ku! ku!*'

The following day, I went with my brother to buy the shoes. Since it was the first time I bought shoes, I did not know my size.

My brother laughed with all his heart when he saw that I was to buy size eight.

'*Khele!* Are you going to wear size *khili?*'

I could not get out of my dream until the minute I saw myself on the road to Seetsa where we were to get the transport to Maseru. My luggage consisted of a white bag that was used for flour, in which I put my dresses and new shoes. Seetsa, the place where we were to get transport to Maseru, was about thirty kilometres from Matsoku. Because I had never worn shoes before, my feet were so cracked that they looked like an old horn. The cracks were as big as dongas.

A long and tedious walk on a rocky, mountainous road made me tired. My feet were swollen and my *litlhabela*, the cracks on my feet, were bleeding. I could hardly walk. My cousin, who was going to do his Form Three in Maseru High School, was used to the walk. He always did the walking and met his Indian teacher at Seetsa. That very man was to take us both from Seetsa in his car to Maseru. I was crying, and my cousin took time to console me and show me that we were left with only a few kilometres to the place. He told me that it was time to rest and eat our provisions. I was afraid that after resting I would not want to continue the journey, but my cousin urged me to rest in order to give him time to nurse my *litlhabela*. I did not know what was going to happen.

My cousin went round to gather some wood and made a big fire. He told me to rub my feet with vaseline and fill the cracks with it. Then, with a warning that I was going to feel excessive pain, he told me to warm my feet in turns, making sure that the vaseline in the cracks was really hot. The pain I felt was almost unbearable, but my cousin encouraged me, saying that my feet would be cured.

After the treatment we sat and ate. My tears were mixed with mucus, and as I did not have a handkerchief, I used the inside of my dress to wipe my face. At that time my cousin was quiet, until the time I stood up to go and pass water. When I came back, he simply said, 'Let us continue; you are now ready to go.'

It was true. My feet felt normal again, and I could walk as I had that morning. We were left with just a short walk to reach

Seetsa. If I were to estimate now, I would say it was just a two-hour walk, compared with the long seven-hour walk from home. When we arrived, the Indian teacher was getting impatient. He had been waiting for thirty minutes and was finding the waiting too long.

Remember, the only vehicle I knew was the truck where people sit in the back. This small one, closed on all sides, with nowhere to sit, gave me a fright. I said to my cousin 'Cousy, are we not going to slip?'

'Slip from what, cousy?'

'Where are we going to sit?'

'Inside.'

The final answer relieved me, because I thought we were going to sit on the hind part of the car with nothing to hold on to. I was so preoccupied with the vehicle that I even forgot to greet the owner. My cousin surprised me. The language he spoke was far from the ordinary. He used the language used at the waters. He told me to put on my shoes and greet the owner of the car.

'What should I say?' I asked.

'Say, "Good afternoon, Sir."'

I said it after him, and when the man replied, I only heard, 'Gedaftne.'

My next problem was getting inside this small thing, tall as I was. My cousin came to my aid. He made sure that I was well seated. He was to occupy the front seat so that he could chat with his teacher, and I was sitting alone on the back seat. Because that was my first experience in a car, cousy suspected that I might get sick and vomit, so he ran to a nearby store and got me a plastic bag, which became handy. When we came to Hlotse, the teacher went to get his things from his friend's house. He came with pills and told me to drink them with a lot of water. I was sitting alone in the back seat, so he told me to use my luggage as a pillow and sleep to avoid the sickness. My cousin reminded me to take off my shoes so as not to dirty the seat.

That part of the journey was so comfortable that I felt I could go on and on. The teacher was going to Maseru High School, so he left us at Lakeside, from where we walked to Thibella, where my sister was staying. When I got out of the car, I could not believe my eyes. Without a second's reflection I said: 'These cars are as many as *Ntate* Thaane's sheep.' And then, 'Look! some are as big as his house. They are like walking houses. *Helang!* look at that one.'

'Cousy, don't worry, you will see them every day. Let's go before it's too late.'

I was so surprised at every turn that I found it hard to pretend I did not see each miracle. So since I could not communicate my surprise to my cousin, I adopted the pig's language.

'Hm!'

I uttered this so often that my cousin had to react. He finally burst with laughter, saying: 'There goes the pig!'

When we arrived at my sister's, she had just come in and was sitting on the bed sorting the things she had bought to prepare supper.

'*Ko-ko!*' we knocked.

'*Kena!* Come in!' she replied carelessly, thinking it was one of her neighbours, only to see enter the so-long-awaited sister. She leaped like a cat at the sight of a rat, embraced me, and showered me with kisses. It was already time for school registration. She told me that the following day I would have to go with her to her work so that she could ask for permission to take me to school for registration. She thanked my cousin, who had to go before it was dark.

That evening was a glorious one for Maleshoane, my niece. She did not do any cooking, because we were to eat the meat and the bread I had brought. It was a big supper of mutton from home. I told them of the long journey we took to Seetsa and how I was crying from sore feet. The fatigue of the long walk came back, and after eating, we all went to bed, and I continued to tell them about home until I could speak no more.

In the morning, I got up, washed myself, dressed up in my new dress, and brought tea to my sister. At the same time I ate my breakfast and got ready for going. The song that my heart sang on the day I brought my sister's letter to *Ntate* Thaane was revived: 'Ku! Ku! Ku!'

There was a long queue waiting to see the principal, a white nun, and we joined it. I had never spoken English with a white person. The only English I knew was that of my primary school teacher. At last my turn came. My heart was beating so hard that the person sitting next to me could hear it. The principal spoke to my sister in Sesotho, and I thought she would do the same to me, but when my turn came, she spoke in English.

'What's your name?'

'Yes.'

'Where do you come from?'

'Form One.'

'Do you know English?'

'Matsoku.'

Not wanting to embarrass me, she transferred me to the secretary, who asked me the same questions in the same order and got correct answers. The secretary asked me why I did not answer them when the sister asked. I told her that I was afraid of the sister. So, that day, I was registered as a Form One student in 'M'abathoana High School.

My school days went on smoothly and at the end of the third year I obtained my second class Junior Certificate. I did not further my studies beyond J.C., because my sister was now educating her own children. She was content because she had given me a basic certificate with which I could find a job; moreover, she had acquainted me with town life, so that I could find my way. So, I looked for a job.

As a worker, I fell in love with a boy who later became the cause of my trouble and separated me from my beloved sister. This same boy was in love with my sister, and I was not aware of their affair. One day when I came back from work, my sister was no more in the eyes, that is, she was unhappy. She showed her anger by her words: 'Two women cannot live in one house. Even wives of a polygamous husband are separated.' She said this going up and down but not wanting to look at me. 'If a person feels that she is a woman, she should find a house where she will live with her man.'

I was puzzled, but still I could not sense the danger. Her daughter, who knew the problem, was waiting for a chance to tell me what was the matter. When I went to the tap to get water, my niece came after me and told me that Thabo, my boyfriend, had

allowed my sister to read a letter which I had written to him. I
still didn't understand. I thought my sister was angry because
she had discovered that I was meddling with a love affair, and, as
a guardian, she was afraid that I might get into trouble.

When I went to work, I told a co-worker what had befallen me
and told her my fears. To my disgust, Mpho told me that she was
afraid to say it before, but now that this had happened, she
wanted me to know that Thabo was also in love with my sister.

Without wasting a minute, I went straight to Thabo and told
him that I 'was no more there with those', meaning that I was
leaving him so that he could pursue his affair with my sister.
However, Thabo went to my sister and insulted her, making her
aware that since she was the mother of a family, he could not
marry her. Thabo further told my sister that she had spoiled his
future with me. This further complicated the matter.

My sister was not happy at all with my presence in her house,
but she was afraid to expel me without informing my brother.
She wrote a letter to my brother, telling him that I was becoming
a burden to her because I did not respect her any more. She told
my brother that when I insult her, the neighbours even have to
come. When my brother heard that, he said, 'I will lash that girl
until she urinates.'

I was not aware of the message, and I was surprised one day
when I came home to find my brother in the house. It was the
first time I met him since I had left home. I rushed to him with
joy, and instead of responding to my joy, he cried. My mind ran
home: 'Is it my sister-in-law who died? Who can it be?' As I was
asking myself these questions, he recovered and was able to
talk.

'Marebetsana, 'M'alisebo called you here to send you to school,
is that not true?'

'It is true, *Ntate*.'

'Are you not grateful for what she has done?'

'I am grateful, *Ntate*.'

'If so, why do you insult her?'

'I have never insulted *Ausi, Ntate*.'

He handed me a letter which was written in *Ausi*'s handwrit-
ing. I opened it and read it.

'*Ntate*, this is not true. I have never insulted *Ausi* 'M'alisebo, and I will never insult her.'

When my sister arrived, my brother told her that he had come to hear my case. My sister said to him: 'Yes, Marebetsana has that habit of insulting me, and one day the neighbours even had to interfere.'

I got so cross that I could not talk but only cry. Maleshoane, my sister's daughter, spoke on my behalf and told her uncle: '*Malome*, it is not true that *mangoane* ever insulted my mother. It is mother who often insults her, and *mangoane* is always quiet.'

My sister said, 'I do not care what she says; I do not want her in my house.' My brother remained in the house until he saw me out of it. My sister kept on saying: 'No two bulls can inhabit the same kraal. I do not want to die the death of the cat.'

I was afraid that she would tell my brother the story of the cat, but my brother was not interested and did not ask. This cat that my sister was talking about died such a tragic death in my hands that I am ashamed to hear it repeated, but since my sister has revealed it, let me tell it in full. I tell it not because I enjoy it, but to show what vengeance can do sometimes.

At the age of six, I was going out with *Ntate*'s shepherds to the veld, and in the evening we would bring mice to roast for supper. That particular day I had killed five. So, as usual, I roasted my meat and told my colleagues to look after them as I was going to the house to get *papa* to eat with the meat. To my great disappointment, when I came back, the cat was swallowing the last piece of my meat. I cried without consolation, but it was a useless cry. The meat was gone. Every time I saw the cat, it was my meat that I saw. So the following day, I told myself that I was going to teach that cat to repent.

'It will know me,' I said.

So that evening, I waited until there was nobody in our sleeping house. Then I took the 'take-me' lamp, which is the lamp made from a jam bottle, filled with paraffin. A long cord passed through the lid into the paraffin. I also took the matches and went out.

'Kitsi, kitsi, kitsi . . . !' I called the cat.

It came, wagging its tail, and in my heart I was saying: 'I will make it repent.'

I took some paraffin and carefully smeared the whole body of the cat with it. I took some soil to wipe the paraffin from my hands. Then I struck a match and lit the cat. In my child's imagination, I thought it would just feel pain. I did not think it was going to die such a hideous death. It tried to extinguish itself on me, but I ran away. Then, with a painful cry, it started running for help. It rubbed its body against a hut with a low thatch. *Lai!* The house was on fire. It ran to a tuft of grass: *lai!* Down to the fields, heap after heap of wheat was alight.

I just had time to get into the house to put the bottle away, and the whole village was moving. Some went to help to extinguish the burning house; others to see the flying fire, because the cat was not walking but flying. Others ran to the fields to stop the fire on the wheat. The cat ran until it fell into the dam. Where I was, I was crying, and when I was asked for the reason, I said I was afraid of that running fire. But in fact I was crying for the cruelty I had done. I was wishing I had not done it, but it was too late. I never told the story to anybody until God made me tell it to my sister when I came to Maseru, so that I could pay for my sin. It was cruel of my sister to refer to this episode at this moment. Why should she think that I could kill her? Or, was she thinking of killing me?

At work, I told my colleagues about my problem, and one lady promised me a room in her house and said it was available immediately. I worried about staying alone in that house, but with the luck of a whistler, when I got home and told my sister that I had found a house and that I was moving tomorrow, she said, 'Why so early? Were you looking for it already?' I did not reply. She turned to my brother and said, 'You see, she was already preparing to go away.'

My brother did not answer. Instead he told me that he wanted to see the owner of the house before he left Maseru. My sister spoke with Maleshoane in a low voice: 'The horse goes with its colt.'

This she said because Maleshoane had told my brother that it was not true that I ever insulted her mother. I was happy when I heard 'M'alisebo's words, because that meant I would have a companion. I would not have had the courage to ask my sister to let Maleshoane come with me; Maleshoane was also happy to come.

The following day we left very early to bring our luggage to the lady's house, and my brother came with us to meet the owner of the house and to pay the rent for the first month. We parted with *Ntate* Thaane and we two went to work while he went back to Matsoku. We enjoyed our stay there without the reprimands of my sister. Even though the owner of the house, as a Mosotho woman, was still casting an eye on us, we started to be freer with our love affairs, which led me into trouble as far as our custom is concerned.

Circumstances forced my fiancé and me to marry without the consent of our parents. His parents were the first to be informed, so that they, in turn, could inform mine. My husband thought of a channel that could be acceptable to his mother, now my mother-in-law. He wrote to his sister, a nun, and explained the whole affair to her. He invited her to meet me so that she could explain and make their mother aware of the already-existing marriage.

The nun, now my sister-in-law, set an appointment. It was in the afternoon around 4:30 p.m., because I was working, though I could not work that day. All the things I typed were full of errors, and that surprised my boss, because he knew me as a good and cautious typist. I cannot explain what was going on in me. I was eager to meet the first member of my new family, besides my husband. Yet I was afraid to meet a nun, of all people. The agitation was: is she going to understand my case, or is she going to rebuke me for immorality? This was because we always take nuns as inhuman and not understanding.

When I came to the convent, where the meeting was scheduled to take place, I was surprised to find the opposite of what I expected. She invited the other sisters to come and see her sister-in-law, and they were all happy, as they all knew my husband as their brother. From that day my anxiety was replaced by tranquillity and contentment that I had joined a family like my own. This family is almost as big as mine, because it has six sons and four daughters. My husband is the third son but the fifth child.

I do not know the approach my sister-in-law took to inform my mother-in-law, but one day when I came back from work, I found a woman I did not know in the house.

'*Lumela 'M'e*,' I greeted the visitor.

'*E, lumela* my child.'

'How do you live, *'M'e?*'

'I live well. How do you live?'

'I also live well.'

I suspected something, because that day my husband was already at home, yet normally he finished work later. Then I was getting ready to go on with my housework when my husband called me back to introduce me officially to his mother.

''*M'e*, this is Julia, my wife.' Then he turned to me and said, 'Julia, this is *'M'e* 'M'arosa, my mother.'

'Come and kiss me, my child,' said the lady. 'From today on you will be called 'M'amothotha.'

'M'e 'M'arosa stayed with me until I delivered my first daughter, who was named 'M'atseliso (Consolation). Since according to the custom the first child was supposed to be born at my home, we quickly sent the message to Matsoku to inform them that I had delivered. They in turn sent their name for the child, which was Lerato (Love). Although because of my work and the distance of my home from the hospital, I chose to bear my child in Maseru, I still owed the customary entrance of the child in my own home.

Lerato was almost two years old when we were finally able to bring her to my home. We sent the message to *Ntate* Thaane to send horses to Mamohau Hospital, the nearest place that could be reached by trucks. But my husband was one of the drivers for the Prime Minister, and just a few days before we started the journey, he got the information that a veterinarian was to go to Bokong to nurse the P.M.'s animals. The doctor was going in a helicopter. My husband asked if we could go with him and he could leave us at Matsoku. He agreed. My husband sent a radio message to tell my brother not to worry about the horses, as we were going to come by helicopter.

This same helicopter used to bring the P.M. to remote places for his community meetings. He had never gone to my village, but people knew that he used *se-roala-nkhoana*, as the helicopter is called in Sesotho. It was a great honour to my brother to learn that his sister was coming home in that manner. Everybody was eager to witness the occasion. They did not know the time when it would come, and every time they heard the sound of a plane they said: 'Tu! tu! tu!', running to the place where they thought it would land. After several rushes, it finally came. I was as anxious as my people. After being away from home for such a long time and after staying in town so long, how would I feel when I got home? How would the people take me?

My village is in a low place between mountains, so before coming to the village, the helicopter appeared from behind a mountain. Looking through the window I could witness the commotion that was taking place. The pilot did not know where to land. He had to go round and round in search of a place, and while he was doing that, people were rushing in all directions. He tried to land on the western side of the village because people were crowded on the eastern side, but when he tried his luck, he found that the plane was too close to the huts. He was afraid to blow off the thatches, so, back he went. Luckily, most of the people were already moving towards the west, thus leaving a space free for landing. He told us to hold ourselves tightly on the seats because he was going to land quickly before the people came back.

He finally succeeded to land, and the wind from the *se-roala-nkhoana* pushed the children, especially, further away. The noise was unbearable: cheers from everyone, dogs barking at this huge thing, donkeys braying in fear of this unfamiliar sound and spectacle. When we climbed out of the helicopter, there were so many cheers that we could not hear ourselves. Some women were crying, asking themselves a question that nobody could answer: 'Why did 'M'athaane die before she could see her daughter arrive home in a helicopter?'

My brother was very happy, and he was going up and down as if reciting poetry, explaining to the people that the woman coming from the *se-roala-nkhoana* is his sister, the very Marebetsana who went to school in Maseru; the man with her is her husband. The children took our luggage and we bade the doctor and the pilot farewell, and off they went.

How She Lost Her Eye

INAHANENG TSEKANA

'I'm falling water from the cliff. I'm a breakable plant. Collect me, Sissy. When I see you, lady, my heart jumps. Allow me to touch you with hands of love,' Lephoqo appealed to Sehlahla. He was the son of the Chief of Malefiloane.

As an experienced herdgirl, Sehlahla often met young men who wanted to be in love with her. She was very beautiful. But my Aunt Sehlahla told me she rejected Lephoqo because she had decided to attend the Circumcision School. She was stimulated to make this choice by her peers, who used to speak humiliating words to her such as, 'You uncircumcised girl, remove this long tail of yours because it makes us stumble and fall.' They mocked her, saying that if she did not go to the Initiation School, she would not be able to satisfy her husband sexually. She said she did not believe these fairy tales.

I asked her, 'My aunt, why did you go to the school if you did not believe them?'

She answered me confidently, 'Son of my sister, don't you know the saying which goes, "Curiosity kills a cat"?'

My aunt had planned to go to the Initiation School on Friday night, when she knew that her father would not be around. The night came without refusing. Sehlahla enclosed the cattle and tethered the horse. She went to the hut and removed the lid of a big three-legged pot. She filled two basins. In the first basin she put *papa* and potatoes. She filled the second basin with *motoho* to the brim. She sat down and munched slowly like a resting ox in the kraal . She did not disclose her intention of going to the Circumcision School to anybody in the family. Even her mother was ignorant of her plan.

When all were asleep, Sehlahla furtively took her clothes and escaped through the door. Tiger, her dog, rose from the kennel. He stretched his legs and wagged his tail in order to meet her. Sehlahla whispered, 'Ha ee, Tiger. Go back and sleep. I'm going nowhere.' The poor dog returned to his kennel, and Sehlahla ran. She tried to hide her footprints by not walking on the footpath. She went as far as the Valley of Witches.

But Tiger was a hunting dog. How could he fail to follow the example of his owner? He rose from the kennel, opened his mouth like a crocodile and wagged his long tail. Within a very short time he had put his nose on the path, following Sehlahla. Her smell could not possibly escape him.

As Sehlahla was walking down the Valley of Witches, her hair stood on end, as though it was pulled by a very strong hand. Everything in her body felt loose. She heard a piercing sound. A person born of a woman could not pass through that valley, known to be the playground of witches and ghosts, without fear. Within a few seconds Sehlahla was surrounded by voices talking randomly. She could not see any people.

'Oh, I was now in a state of consternation like a hart tied to the stake and surrounded by dogs,' she told me.

Then the noise intensified: hummm . . . hui-hoi-hoooi! This sound vibrated in her ears painfully. Sehlahla felt as if the earth could open up and swallow her. Finally she ran. Unfortunately, she kicked a stone and fell on a sharp-edged rock which wounded her in the thigh. Immediately, the red liquid began to ooze from her thigh. The hideous noise never stopped: huuuu . . . huii . . . When she arose, Sehlahla saw a tall, white, bony thing. Nobody could fathom how tall it was. Unswervingly, it came toward her. She shouted,

'Mother – 'M'e Marina, help! Your child is dying.' At that moment, she heard Tiger barking hopelessly: Au! Au! A-uuu!

'Oh, poor Tiger. He has lost track of me.' Then she cried out, 'Tiger, Tiger! Help me –'.

Even before Sehlahla completed her sentence she was hit by a heavy iron on the head and she fell down. She saw a thousand stars passing before her eyes. Unconscious of what had happened to her, Tiger came nearer and barked joyfully. Sehlahla did not rise. Tiger put his legs on her back and scratched her a little. Sehlahla rose and cleared her throat and thanked Tiger gladly.

The Circumcision School was still a bit far. At dawn Sehlahla saw a light flickering some distance ahead of her. She was still shivering from cold and fear. She took shelter in a cave, waiting for the sun to rise so that she could move on toward the school. Her teeth were beating against each other in rhythm, as if she were singing a well-rehearsed song.

'But,' she continued her tale, 'the sun never disappointed me. I therefore advanced to the school.'

On her arrival, she was met by Korina, the keeper of the girls. Korina took her to 'M'ahlamini, the owner of the school. Then Sehlahla said to me, laughing, 'That 'M'ahlamini was a fat woman. Her small head was drowned in wrinkles of fat. Son of my sister, wait until you see her walking. I mean she was round all over. When she walked, it was as if a big rock was rolling. Oh, I used to pity that woman.'

I was not interested in the description of 'M'ahlamini. I vehemently interrupted her: '*Mangoane* Sehlahla, stop telling us about the nature of that witch. I want to know how you happened to lose your right eye.'

'Don't hurry for the soup before the meat is cooked thoroughly,' she said.

Sehlahla's going to the school without her parents' permission was unceremonious. 'M'ahlamini knew Sehlahla's parents very well, so she informed them. However until Sehlahla's parents could give a response, Sehlahla was not allowed to mix with the other girls; she was kept in a secluded place. Her heart was longing to see and meet the other students, but she waited. When a young girl joined the Circumcision School, parents were supposed to legitimize that commitment by accompanying her and promising to support her with money, food and clothing while she attended the school.

On the third day, at around three o'clock in the afternoon, Korina summoned Sehlahla. She told me that her heart at that time began to beat faster. She was murmuring these encouraging words to herself: 'I know. It would not be my mother if she has not bought me a new dress and shoes. I'm sure my mother will not disappoint me.' Indeed, she was very excited, so much that she had forgotten her father's negative attitude towards her.

When Korina saw the joy shining on Sehlahla's face, she refrained from telling the girl immediately that her parents wanted their child to return home. After a lapse of three hours, Korina gave Sehlahla meat and papa and ordered her to eat quickly. My aunt asked Korina with surprise, 'Why should I eat quickly? Am I missing a lot by not attending the practice today?'

Korina answered, bending her head to the ground and whispering softly, 'Oh, no, my child. You have to go back home –'. Korina did not finish her last word before she was interrupted by Sehlahla's probing questions.

'Me going home? For what? I'm refusing. I want to be a woman.' Sehlahla burst into tears. She screamed so loudly that 'M'ahlamini and other students heard. 'M'ahlamini was very disappointed to see that Sehlahla was firm in her decision. 'M'ahlamini empathised with Sehlahla, especially because she knew how stubborn Sehlahla's father was. Then 'M'ahlamini spoke, 'You are not going, my child.'

'M'ahlamini decided to incorporate Sehlahla into the school. However, 'M'ahlamini was not in a position to support Sehlahla for the six months' duration. 'M'ahlamini supplied Sehlahla with old clothes: a patchy blanket full of holes as if rats had fed themselves on it.

'Oh! you should have seen my back,' Sehlahla disclosed to me. 'My arse was left uncovered as though it was peeping out, looking for a piece of cloth to cover its shame.' She ate little, and that only after the others had eaten. After three months her cracked and furrowed feet were tangible evidence that they had not known shoes for that long. Those very feet used to spill the dew and scatter the snow each morning when they were going to collect wood. Sehlahla began to be dissatisfied with the school.

One day as Sehlahla perched on a rock trying to warm herself, her mind went back to a time when she used to wake up at dawn to drive the cattle from the paddock into the veld. It was Sehlahla's custom to kindle fire in order to warm herself from the chilling winter wind. It also came into Sehlahla's mind how her father, Chaka, used to thrash her for unreasonable things. Marina, Sehlahla's mother, could not intervene because her husband considered her a wife or a human being only at the flashing of the lightning. She was absolutely nothing in the family.

As Sehlahla was viewing her life in retrospect, her mind could not easily forget the time there was a quarrel, to the effect that Chaka denied that Sehlahla was his child. This quarrel took months in the family.

'In fact Chaka, my father, was on the brink of divorcing my mother. My heart was painful, but I did not know what to do. I was seven years old at that time,' she said, bitterly. 'That is why I was named Sehlahla.' The word *sehlahla* means bush, and in Manganeng, it is common to associate illegitimate children with bushes because their fathers are not known. People say: 'You are from the bush tribe.'

However, the long argument over the illegitimacy of Sehlahla's birth was resolved by Chaka's elder brothers. They convinced Chaka that Sehlahla's fingers, feet and face were the same as his.

In Sehlahla's family there were six in all – four boys and two girls. Sehlahla was the first-born, and she was followed by four boys. Three of these four boys were attending Mateanong Primary School. It was Chaka's ideology that he could not educate his daughters because when they were married they were going to enrich the in-laws with their knowledge. Chaka's philosophy differed from the culture and the values of the other villagers of Manganeng. In that village girls were supposed to go to school while boys were to be herdboys or shepherds. It was rare that boys could be found within the four walls of the classroom. One can imagine how Sehlahla felt as a full-time herdgirl.

'I used to fight with boys, using sticks and stones,' she remarked. However, she had learned and accepted that life.

As she sat on the rock, she thought of many things. Her friends and enemies passed before her eyes. She also remembered that when she was about to leave her lovely village of Manganeng, Lephoqo was in pursuit of marrying her. But there was no spark in her heart to be married by Lephoqo. Immediately her mind shifted as she remembered her mother and how Marina used to kindle fire for Sehlahla. As Sehlahla was thinking about this, a song came to her mind. Sehlahla sang it softly,

> *Marina 'm'e oa ka*   Marina, my mother,
> *ke ha tseetse;*   I am very cold;
> *mpepe ka thari*   put me on your back
> *ke tle ke futhumale.*   so that I may warm myself.
> *Ke ha tseetse;*   I am very cold;
> *bona mali a rotha*   look, the blood is oozing
> *maotong a ngoana oa hau;*   from your daughter's feet;
> *mo koietse a robale.*   rock her till she sleeps.

As Sehlahla clasped her hands and sorrowfully sang the song, a yellow warm liquid involuntarily flowed from her inner thighs to her frozen feet. *Ao* shame! She was trying to warm herself. Sehlahla felt as if her mother were washing her with warm water from a black three-legged pot. Sehlahla unintentionally stretched her hands to hug her loving mother. As she lifted her head to the sky, Sehlahla's eyes met the fierce eyes of the king of the mountains, Eagle. Eagle was flying just above her head, at a distance of about a stone's throw. She closed her eyes and thought that it would be better to be swallowed by Eagle than to die in the hands of 'M'ahlamini. Her heart, which was beating very fast, recited a poem:

> Oh bird of great valleys and mountains,
> your habitation is next to the sun.
> I know you have come for me and me alone.
> Why tarry? I am already worn out.
> Sustain me with your strong feathers
> and take me nearer to the sun
> that's my home.

Even before Sehlahla could finish the poem, she fell unconscious, and thereafter she did not know what happened.

The following day Sehlahla found herself in 'M'ahlamini's hut. A fire made of cow dung and *cheche* wood was built next to her. Korina was massaging animal fats into her open wounds and also massaging Sehlahla's whole body with fats to facilitate the circulation of blood. Gradually, Sehlahla recovered.

Casting her eyes towards the hillock, Sehlahla saw her age-mates playing hide-and-seek. They were all nude, enjoying the warmth of the sun, which came seldom. Sehlahla used to play the game when she was a herdgirl. As she was watching, she wanted to jump into the arena with them. But how could it be? Sehlahla's feet would not carry her because they were so swollen.

Suddenly, Sehlahla saw Nthabi running like a fox chased by vicious dogs. Nthabi was running down the hill screaming, 'Help! Help! Help!'

The game stopped. All eyes were watching Nthabi, but they did not see anything chasing her. Nthabi ran like a madman chasing wind. Arriving at the hut, she collapsed and became unconscious for about five minutes. 'M'ahlamimi was summoned. On her arrival she noticed a wound on Nthabi's leg and then shouted, '*Basali ba Bafokeng*, this child has been bitten by a python.'

The place where Nthabi had been playing was notorious for snakes and dangerous reptiles in summer. But snakes usually hibernate in winter, so they were surprised that there could be snakes at this time of the year. Korina examined the wound again closely. After touching the wound, Korina shouted, 'This child has not been bitten by a snake, but by a hyena. Please let's call Mocholoko, the traditional doctor.'

It is the custom of the Basotho at Manganeng to have a traditional doctor nearby when girls are at the Circumcision School. The principal job of this man is to guard the students against witchcraft and lightning, and to teach the students how to use herbs to heal various diseases such as headaches, flu, etc.

On arrival, Mocholoko, a stalwart man, was panting like a bulldog in the sunshine. His head was covered with the wings of eagles, ostriches and vultures. Around his neck he had tied many cords and an ostrich egg. He had two horns on his shoulders. He wore a blanket made of skins of foxes, hyenas and harts. Besides that, he had a huge leather bag filled with bones of different animals. He was fearsome indeed.

Mocholoko opened his bag and took from it a black substance, *mohlabelo*, which he smeared on the Nthabi's wound before applying fats of hyena. As Nthabi was recovering, Mocholoko dug his hands into his bag. His right hand was full of bones which he spread on the ground. He praised these bones:

> *Masapo a tse shoeleng malaola tse phelang.*
> *Masapo a ho kokonoa ke ntjana hlabana.*
> (Bones of the dead, instruct the living;
> bones to be eaten by the dog.)

He cast lots to find the person who had sent that hyena. My aunt was watching all these things carefully.

Early the next morning all the students were told to queue in accordance with their ethnic groups. Since Sehlahla was of the Bafokeng clan, she came first. Mocholoko took a black substance and said he was going to smear it on their foreheads to guard against evil spirits. When Mocholoko was about to smear my aunt, he hesitated, seeming to brood over something gigantic. He went back to 'M'ahlamini, and they whispered together. Thereafter, Mocholoko continued with his task. On completion, all students were dismissed save Sehlahla.

Korina called Sehlahla to her hut and told Sehlahla that she had to repay the two days she spent without collecting wood by completing a special task. Korina was very excited. She put her hand on Sehlahla's shoulder and commented, 'You are a good girl.' It was Sehlahla's first time to see Korina smiling. Sehlahla was surprised to see that Korina had black gums and palate, and that she had only one tall tooth in her upper gums.

'When she laughed she reminded me of the face of a dead dog left in the cold for many days. I tell you, son of my sister, you could not stand looking at her.' However Sehlahla went away and resumed her task. Since she was a strong girl, she finished her work quickly and joined the others.

Sehlahla found them making Basotho hats, using *loli* grass. She regretted that she had missed a number of lessons. In fact she wanted to be trained in cooking and in the art of smearing the floor. During her childhood as a shepherd, she never had time to cook or smear the floor or the house walls. Nevertheless she continued, learning how to make a hat. Within no time she had grasped the techniques and was teaching other girls. When the training was over they went to sleep.

In the middle of the night she had a dream in which she saw a short, muscular man approaching her. This man had covered his face with something like a blanket. Softly and appealingly this man whispered to Sehlahla, 'Now you are going to marry me, Sehlahla. You have wasted precious moments. Today you are not going to escape. It is hard to run away from the facts of love. Kiss me now, and love will be complete.' As this man was stretching his hands to touch her, Sehlahla immediately rose from the bed and shouted angrily, '*Hei*, you monkey, *ha ke u batle*. I don't want you. You are not going to marry me. I cannot be married to stinking herdboys.'

From that day Sehlahla never had any rest. She was haunted by fear day and night. During the night while sleeping she would hear voices, but she saw no one. Sehlahla also felt that 'M'ahlamini and Korina had changed in their behaviour toward her.

Sehlahla tried to repress these thoughts by mingling with other students. Still, something told her that something terrible was going to happen to her. As the fear intensified within her, Sehlahla sometimes became hysterical and pleaded for mercy, 'Please do not kill me. Allow me to see my mother and father again.' She would say that twice or thrice a day. Other students were confounded; some thought she was mad.

'One night as I was sleeping,' she explained, 'somebody came to my bed and sprinkled some powder on my face, and from that time I did not know what happened.' As she told me this part of the story, tears began to run down her cheeks. She fell silent for a long time and then told me she wanted to stop telling the story because it was piercing her heart. She only continued when I assured her that I needed the information because I wanted to write a story about her. Hesitantly, she proceeded: 'When I became conscious, I found myself fastened to a tree in the forest. I could smell blood. I looked up, and there was Mocholoko, leering over me, his dagger in his hand. I screamed, squirmed and kicked, but in vain. Boldly Mocholoko pushed his dagger and plucked out my eye and threw it into his bag.'

As Mocholoko was about to cut Sehlahla's private parts, he heard a person coughing. He picked up his bag and asked his feet to carry him. He ran so fast that within a few seconds his steps could not be heard.

'I was left there alone, the blood dripping from my eye staining the ground. I screamed till my voice left me. But no one came to my rescue. Around twelve o'clock noon, I saw two men passing by. I pleaded for help. Fortunately they listened to my cry,' my aunt told me sorrowfully.

She eventually learned that the plot to kill her was suggested by the Chief of Malefiloane. Since Sehlahla had refused his son Lephoqo, he sent Mocholoko to kill her. Mocholoko was able to influence 'M'ahlamini to allow him to murder Sehlahla because her parents had been irresponsible.

This suited Mocholoko because he was going to select important parts of Sehlahla's body for the consolidation of his medicine and the strengthening of his cult. That is why he started with an eye.

'After the men untied me,' Sehlahla continued, 'I went straight home. My mother could not believe what stood before her; she thought she was dreaming. She ran to me and hugged me. But my mother wept bitterly when realising that I was one-eyed. There was no need to weep. It had happened.'

A Letter to 'M'e

MOROESI AKHIONBARE

April 5, 1993

'M'e,

You were my best friend since I was a little girl . . . You told me that even though I was excited about learning how to knit, I should not rush to do it so soon after waking up – before the house had been cleaned. I suppose that is why I can never cook in a dirty kitchen.

I remember what we did, and the stories you told me as we cooked and cleaned house:

About your courting days and early marriage with my father, *Ntate*. How you woke up at the crack of dawn to confront a woman you suspected of having an affair with him. You went to the servants' quarters where she stayed and lured her out of her room with a friendly voice.

She came out in her white, starched uniform and stood with you among the puddles of last night's rain. How, without much conversation, you fell upon her with fists and started dragging her in the mud, dirtying her white clothes. And then you walked away, having made your point.

The story of Dr Jacques, the white doctor who used to go early to Sunday Mass, leaving his wife asleep. How, when she scolded him for not waking her up to go along, he told her that whenever the Lord called either of them in death, neither would be able to bring the other along.

My younger sister, 'M'amarame, was assigned the duty of fetching a bottle of fresh milk early every morning from Rev. Makhetha's home. One day she complained, ''M'e, I don't see why

I should be the one to pick up milk every day; besides, I don't eat milk!'

'Yes, my dear daughter,' you said, 'that is why I send YOU, because I can trust you. If I sent the ones who eat milk, they might drink it on the way!'

How, that tragic night 'M'amarame died in a car accident, *Ausi* described the condition of the car after the accident, and you spent the whole night praying that God would take 'M'amarame's soul rather than let her live the life of a vegetable. *Ausi* feared the effect the full truth might have on your own frailness that night.

The tale of a child in the Free State farms who cried endlessly, nagging her mother to get her the egg from an ostrich that seemed to lie dead in the veld. The mother finally put her hand up the bird's behind, trying to reach the egg.

The ostrich woke up and started running, dragging the mother behind it. And running yet harder, tightening its behind around the mother's irritating hand. The frightened child wailed behind the cloud of dust, 'Mother, please come back! I don't want the egg any more!'

In later years, when you could no longer work as a stay-in maid, you used to pick up the laundry of a white bachelor to wash and iron at home. One day he complained that you were tearing the collars of his shirts. How you told him there and then, that his shirts would from that day last him forever, because you would not be picking up his washing any more.

How, because of walking to the 'kitchens'* at dawn in all sorts of weather, you finally developed a bad back, forcing you to walk with a slow stoop, aided by a walking stick.

And the sores that developed in your armpits and thighs when Dr Clarke tied your waist with a corset of plaster for six winter months. How your body inside the plaster used to itch, and you asked us to scratch it with a ruler.

Helping you wash your back in later years, I noticed a depression on your spine, and I knew that you must have slipped a spinal disc carrying one or another of your lifetime burdens.

* Homes of whites where Basotho women worked as cooks and cleaners.

You got raving mad when 'M'a-Dambuza, that crazy old woman who wore a doek like a hood over her head, spitting into a tin, asked whether your back was bent because of a heavy weight of sins. How you retorted that your load had to be very heavy, since you were carrying both your sins and hers!

Towards the end you developed a bad heart, and were treated by a German doctor at Roma Hospital. How, when you knew that a hospital stay could no longer do you any good, you begged us to bring you home.

The day *Ausi* picked you up, you joyfully walked around the ward, bidding the other patients good-bye, telling them that you were going home 'to see my chicks!' Us, your children. One patient lamented, '*Nkhono*, where will I get a second portion of food when you are gone?'

Tonight you sound restless and in pain. I want to come and comfort you, and perhaps say a prayer. But the baby 'M'amonoto is equally restless, whining, crying, and will not sleep. Finally we all fall asleep.

In the morning, my brother, Victor, comes in before we are awake. You are also still resting. He is concerned by the tilt of your head; he touches your feet. They are cold. He summons us to your bedside, and we all agree that you are no more . . .

Why was I not allowed the gift of at least sharing a last prayer with you, which would have been my way of saying a fond goodbye to you, my dearest friend and mentor?

Many of my friends did not come for your funeral, because they thought you were just a grandmother. They did not know that I could never have need for more support than you gave me; that you had, on your frail back, carried two generations of children who knew none other as 'M'e.

Your daughter,
Ketsi

Catastrophe

GUGULETHU S. DLAMINI

As I walked down the hospital corridor following a white-uniformed nurse to the exit, I felt pain all over: pain in my legs, pain in my head, pain in my stomach, pain in my breast, pain in my knees, pain everywhere and pain all over. The pain that bothered me most was the one I felt in my heart. I felt like crying out aloud. I was bitter against the world. I hated the nurses in that hospital. I felt bitter against the women that were hugging and suckling their babies contentedly. I thought, at least they have what they wanted. One step after the other was a trauma. I never imagined such pain and bitterness were possible.

I do not remember signing my name as we reached the desk at the exit, but I know I did, because everyone does it as a rule. At the exit my brother was waiting patiently for me. He took the baby from the nurse and mumbled something to which I did not respond.

Outside the hospital the sun was so bright it seemed to be mocking my mood, because I was feeling so low and so dark inside. I remember I heard some laughter coming from the out-patient department of the hospital, and that made me really angry. I thought people had no right to be happy when I was this depressed.

I sat on the passenger's seat holding my baby against my lap. I did not look at her face. I knew I did not feel anything for her. She had already caused me so much trouble and pain. As we drove home, we passed some schoolboys and girls walking down the road, chatting cheerfully. I guessed they were my age, about thirteen to fourteen. I envied them; I wished I were there with them and not here, feeling the way I did. My brother drove silently, avoiding looking at me; instead he concentrated on the road. I guess he could tell I was not in the mood for talking. I felt very grouchy.

At home my Aunts Zodwa and Thola were waiting excitedly outside. As soon as the car stopped, they flew to the passenger's door, opened it, took the baby and started asking questions, none of which I answered. I just proceeded straight to my bedroom and lay down quietly. I noticed changes in the room which annoyed me: there was a new cot, a white chest of drawers, and some brightly-coloured things for the baby. I did not like the new look of my bedroom. It seemed already crowded and disorderly.

I wished the pain and baby would go away. I thought quietly, 'Lord, why should it be me? Why didn't someone tell me it would be like this? Why was I so naïve? So stupid?'

I blamed myself for letting this happen to me. I blamed my mother for not being open and freely discussing sex with me. I blamed the school for not teaching sex education as part of the curriculum. I blamed Zulu culture for being the way it is. I believed if I was from other societies and cultures, where sex and childbirth are an open subject, or at least where abortion is legal, things would not have been this way.

As I was lying there, I vowed to myself that I would live the rest of my life the way I want to live. I would do what I think is best for me and never let myself be talked into doing anything that I do not believe in. With that vow, I drifted slowly into a fitful sleep.

It all began during the 1977 June vacation. Maybe I should not have stayed back at school during that vacation. I should have gone home with my brother when the schools closed. But I desperately wanted to be a member of the camping crew that was going to the Crocodile Camping Site near Scottburgh, on the Natal South Coast. Among the crew was my best friend, Queen, and we were the only two juniors. Most of the crew was composed of seniors. We were to stay at the camp site for a week and help with the outdoor cleaning campaign organised to 'Keep South Africa Clean'.

On the fourteenth of June our school crew, together with some students from Amangwane High and Ukhahlamba High, the neighbouring schools, left for the South Coast at around 9:30 in the morning. Most of the students were well acquainted, because they were classmates and age-mates. We noticed we were the only two left out. So to avoid being nuisances and targets for everyone's little errands, we decided to sit on the back seat of the bus. It was nicer, for everyone was in front of us and we could see all of them. Another advantage was that we were far from the three teachers who were travelling with us.

People were chatting in pairs or groups of four or five, and we began singing and chanting loudly. There was one song which seemed to last forever. It went:

Shosholoza!	Roll
Shosholoza!	Roll
Kulezontaba	Into those mountains
Sitimela	Train
Sigond'e mampondweni.	Headed for Pondoland.

We reached the South Coast at around three o'clock in the afternoon. There were already three other buses from different districts in Natal. We were allocated sleeping chalets, two to each. I shared mine with Queen. A welcome party was organised for the same night, and the cleaning programme was scheduled to commence on the next morning. The party was meant to welcome us as well as give us a chance to get to know one another.

The party was held at the main hall. This was my first experience of a party other than the local, boring birthday parties we always attended at home. I was very excited, and Queen thought it was wonderful. Some older girls were dressed to kill, in stockings, high-heeled shoes, jewellery and all. I remember Queen whispering to me, 'Look at this one, she can't even walk properly. I wonder why she wore those high heels.'

We giggled and started dancing crazily to the music. Some boys came and introduced themselves to us and danced with us. We tired of their company and excused ourselves, pretended we were going outside, but just disappeared in the crowd and hid away from those boys.

The second pair of boys that approached us was really dazzling. We liked them. They were cute, tallish; one was dark and handsome, the other was light and attractive. Mine was Thamie and Queen's was Sandile. We danced with them for the rest of the evening.

After the party, they escorted us to the chalet. It became a routine for the whole week. Most of the time we never met during the day, because we were divided into groups and worked in different places. We only met for supper at the dining hall. Each evening our boys would sit with us and then escort us to our chalet.

On Friday the 19th of June, it was the last day of the cleaning session, and a farewell party was organised for us. This party also began at 7:00 p.m. The party was more relaxed and jolly than the first one. Everyone had loosened up and was well acquainted with everyone else. For Queen and me the week had been the most exciting of our lives. We had been to real parties, and now we had boyfriends – things which were taboo for us at home and at school. Here, things were different. No one really bothered what we did. In fact we started kissing those boys on Wednesday. I remember we talked about it long after the chalet lights were turned off.

At the party we danced a little, had some soft drinks, and then the boys suggested we all go back to their chalet. We suggested our own. The boys agreed and we all left. On our way to our room there were couples of boys and girls talking under the trees, some leaning against the walls. We just proceeded straight to our destination. We sat talking and laughing until the lights were turned off. We asked the boys to go. But they insisted on staying. That is when it all happened.

When the schools reopened in July, we went back to school. I did not feel any different. I only noticed that I had gained weight. Towards the end of August I remember Martha and Ethel whispering in the showers.

'See! I told you.'

'I haven't noticed anything.'

'Look closely. I think it's true.'

I did not really care what they were saying; I wasn't interested in gossip. In fact I did not think anything was wrong with me. Moreover I was still menstruating normally, and that was the only symptom of pregnancy I knew.

Some of the girls were even brave enough to question me. 'Nonhlanhla, you seem to have gained weight so much. What's wrong with you?' inquired Nomsa one day.

'I don't know,' I replied innocently.

They laughed out loud. Still I was not bothered. It was only at the end of October that I missed my period. Then I began to panic. I realised I could be pregnant. Queen, on the other hand, seemed normal. She hadn't gained weight. She did not look anxious or anything. I was scared even to discuss the issue with her. I just hoped it was not true.

It was 17 November when the hostel matron called me to her office and asked me to go and see the doctor. She handed me a note that I was supposed to give to the doctor. Though I was curious to know what was in the letter, I didn't dare open it. The doctor thoroughly checked me and scribbled something for me to give to the matron. The temptation to tear the letter open was even greater, but I did not.

At school the matron took the letter and sent me back to class. The following day my mother came to school. Now I was sure that I was pregnant. She looked at me once, and tears welled in her eyes. I started crying also. I was so scared. I was especially scared of my father. My mother went into the principal's office. I went back to class, but I could not concentrate; I was distracted; I felt so lonely and lost. I even noticed for the first time that most of the girls had recently started avoiding me.

At lunch my mother told me not to worry. She said the principal had allowed me to stay at school until the end of the exams, which was a week away. That was the worst week I had lived through. I contemplated suicide, but I didn't know how to go about it. I thought of an abortion, but I knew it was illegal and I might go to jail. When the exams ended I dreaded going home, yet I knew I had to go.

My father came to take me home. I didn't dare look him in the eyes. I was so scared, I thought he might kill me. He did not say anything, though. He just took my luggage, talked to the principal and the matron, and then we drove straight home in total silence. I never noticed Amanzimtoti, Umkomaas, Doonside and Ifafa, the small towns I love so much; nor the palm trees and a series of beaches that border the South Coast. I was just looking straight ahead of me, dreading the rest of my whole life.

At home Fanny, my dog, came bouncing towards us, flapping her long ears and wagging her tail happily. But I just ignored her and walked straight to the kitchen door. My mother and brother were waiting for us. Lunch was ready on the table. There was a lovely aroma of roast beef in the air, but I still had no appetite. I picked at my food with downcast eyes. I could tell that everyone was trying his best to be cheerful and talk enthusiastically. The conversation covered everything except my pregnancy.

Everyone made an effort to cheer me up. All the members of my family were there for me. My brother, who was then sixteen, two years older than me, became my best friend. He was always with me. I could tell he was feeling sorry for me, but he did not discuss my state. On Christmas Eve everyone went to church. I couldn't go. I felt cut out of the whole society. When schools reopened and my brother had to go, I felt like I was the only person in the world.

Sometimes I could tell that my mother wanted to say something to me, but as soon as she sat down next to me, tears welled in her eyes and she would stand up and busy herself with something else. My father never said anything either. I guess the whole situation of tenseness and discomfort stemmed from our culture. Zulu parents never discuss sex with their children. Even older people amongst themselves don't talk about sex. March came, and I went to the hospital to give birth.

Postscript

Nonhlanhla is now past thirty years old and unmarried. She and her daughter, who attends the University of Durban-Westville, stay together and are very loving friends. Nonhlanhla qualified as a teacher, and she is now employed as a sex educator by a governmental health unit. She says, 'If I could help it, no teenager would go through what I went through.'

The Decision to Remain

MAPHELEBA LEKHETHO

'Tell me the truth, woman, who scratched your face so horribly like this?' *Ntate* Thabo asked *'M'e* 'M'akena with amazement and fury.

'Oh, *Ntate* Thabo, my dear husband, it is the Zulus in Durban – I mean the factory and railway workers, my master; that is to say, the people who were on strike,' *'M'e* 'M'akena reported with a quivering voice.

'Hei! *Mosali!* did they beat you up for nothing? Tell me, you fool, a daughter of a witch, or were you beaten by men – I mean your husbands?' *Ntate* Thabo inquired, as his face blushed with rage and he slapped her roughly on the cheek.

'Nta . . . Nta . . . Nta . . . te . . . Thabo, please believe me. I can't lie to you. Oh, *basali*, he has finished me!' *'M'e* 'M'akena cried out as she fell down, as the blood oozed through her nose onto the floor.

'M'e 'M'akena had narrowly escaped death from the strikers in Durban who were on the look-out to punish or even to kill anybody who seemed not to support their struggle against low wages. The strikers shouted for solidarity from fellow blacks to fight the white monster. In order to save her life, *'M'e* 'M'akena ran away homeward from the complexities of the city.

'M'e 'M'akena had earned some prosperity, marked by an array of household utensils, two beds, and a wardrobe. She also had many clothes for her nine children. Despite all the things that aunt had brought home, her husband was impossible to please.

Ntate Thabo never expressed any compassion or sympathy for his wife. Nor did he show any appreciation of her success demonstrated by the possessions she brought home. One night while sitting by the fire aunt told me: 'Your Uncle Thabo, to whom I tried my best to be subservient and faithful as a king's servant, was as aggressive and domineering as Makoanyane, that old Mosotho warrior you learned about in history. My husband was a lion,' *'M'e* 'M'akena said with bitterness.

'Did he ever beat you up, aunt?' I asked foolishly.

'Child of my brother, my body was always in pain,' she continued. 'But one day he struck me so many times that I fainted. Thank God, he ran away afterwards, thinking that I was dead.'

Her husband returned the following night with a group of men who were heavily armed, and they took away all of the valuable property that aunt had bought. It was sheer luck that aunt and the children were sleeping in another hut nearby.

'And so I told my children, who were militant and wanted to shout, to be quiet lest they be killed.'

After that night, *'M'e* did not see *Ntate* Thabo for about three years, and it was during those years that she was accused of witchcraft.

'Hee! Setho, child of my brother, when you want to marry, my word to you is, please ask God to guide you to the right life partner. I don't want to see the wife of my brother die young of heart attack because of these green girls that you boys marry.'

'Why do you say so, aunt?' I asked.

'My child, haven't I told you that I appeared before Chief Seahle's court one day, mmm? *Moshanyan'a ka*, my little boy, happenings of this world are difficult to understand. 'M'amotse-lisi, the wife of my eldest son, said that I bewitched, and thus was responsible for the death of, her first child who passed away at birth,' aunt said in a low voice.

'And so you were fined?' I asked.

'Hee . . . Setho, when you fear, you should fear God,' aunt said as she sighed. 'Well, the Lord was good to me. All the village people stood behind me.'

'*'Khele!*' they said, almost in a chorus, 'We know 'M'akena is a deeply religious woman, and we have been living with her all these years. We have never heard even a fool accusing her or even suspecting her of practising witchcraft.'

'*'M'e* 'M'apulane, an elderly woman, said with a sharp and

commanding voice, 'Hei *ngoananyana, se ka tla bapala ka rona mona! Rea tseba here uena u matha le bo kherenkhoa bana kaofela. Ha ho na mosali ea tsoanang le 'M'akena ka boikokobetso lerato, borapeli le mosa.'* (Hei little girl, don't play with us here. We know that you go from one divine healer to another seeking herbs. There is none of all the women who are here, who is as humble, loving, religious and kind as 'M'akena.)

The court was dismissed, and at the end of the day 'M'amotselisi was fined eighty *maloti* for defaming the character of 'M'e 'M'akena.

Not all was well, however, because around the time of the trial, aunt lost her job. She says of that time, 'Poverty threw itself into my family. I tried everything to combat the destitution which befell my house. I even thought that maybe God had forsaken me. But there is a saying that we inherited from our ancestors, child of my brother –'. Aunt paused, wiped her eyes, and looked far away.

'What is it, *Rakhali?*' I asked, fearing she had lost interest in telling me.

'It is that children of the same father help one another: one kills a wild animal, another offers his animal, and the last collects fire with an old piece of clay pot,' aunt said.

'What is that supposed to mean, aunt?' I inquired, more puzzled than before she had told me the saying.

'My child, your father! I will never forget the favour he did me at that time.' Again she kept silent for a while. This time I sat with her in the silence and waited. 'May God rest his soul, that child of Chief Mankoe,' she said.

'What did he do?' I finally could contain my curiosity no longer.

'M'e 'M'akena told me that my father paid exorbitant school fees for *Abuti* Teboho, her fourth son, as she could not afford to keep him in school. *Abuti* Teboho was going to do Form A at Eagle's Peak High School, after passing Standard Seven with distinction at Tsoelike Primary. *Ntate* Sekhonyana also lent aunt four oxen for ploughing her fields, as this was the ploughing season.

At that moment *Ntate* Thabo showed up again after his

three-year absence, but he never explained himself, and aunt never asked him to. Nor did he bother to plough the fields. Instead, aunt explained, 'He would move from one drinking place to another, boasting that he was now a man like other men, because he had cattle.'

Aunt herself ploughed all her three fields, mainly with the help of her child, Motlalepula, whose name means one-who-brings-rain. 'M'achone and Letlatsa were still in primary school, but they also helped by going to school on alternate days and helping in the fields on the days when they didn't go to school.

The maize and sorghum that aunt got from the fields was barely enough for her nine children, her husband, and herself. Before the winter came to an end, they had run out of food. *Ntate* Sekhonyana, my father, sent a food offering and took four of aunt's sons to live in his household.

Instead of being grateful for the relief, Ntate Thabo accused my aunt: "'M'akena, *mosali oa ka, u ntlotholotse.* (Makena, my wife, you have let me down.) What kind of man will people say I am? A man who fails to support his family, and gives out his children to his in-laws?"

Aunt paid dearly with her body as *Ntate* Thabo beat her time and again for the four children who were staying with her brother. One night after drinking, at around one o'clock in the morning, *Ntate* Thabo beat her mercilessly and commanded her to go out in the night to bring back his children.

He shouted, '*Hei uena mosali tooe! Ke batla bana ba ka moo! Hona joale. Ha ke na bana ba lulang bohoeng. Kapa ha ke utloahale?*' (Hey you woman! I want my children here! And now. I don't have children who live with my in-laws, or am I not heard?) He completed his last word with a heavy blow across aunt's shoulders.

She ran to the place of her intimate friend, '*M'e* 'M'atsepo, who was also her churchmate. '*M'e* 'M'atsepo was living at Ha Mosuoe, a village about five kilometres from Tsoelike. It was around three a.m. when '*M'e* Makena started knocking on '*M'e* 'M'atsepo's door. Aunt was trembling with fear and shivering with cold, as winter was gradually coming on. Aunt had run all the way barefooted, in a very light night dress.

Ko! Ko-ko! my aunt knocked and called her friend's name. She got no response from her friend, but *'M'e* 'M'atsepo's two dogs were barking loudly and were about to attack aunt when Khethang, 'M'atsepo's herdboy, rushed out of his hut to beat the supposed thief. To his dismay he saw *'M'e* 'M'akena, and he quickly controlled the dogs. By this time, aunt was shouting at the top of her voice, 'Haiee! Haiee! Haiee! 'M'atsepo, 'M'atsepo, *thusetsa hle mosali!'* (Help me, woman!)

Finally 'M'atsepo woke from her deep sleep, and when she got to the door, she was perplexed. She exclaimed, '*Khethang, moshanyana ka,* (Khethang, my son) what is it that I see with my own eyes? Are my eyes telling me the truth?'

Before Khethang could utter any word, *'M'e* 'M'akena said, ''M'atsepo, *se ka tsoha, ke 'na hle mosali.'* (Don't be afraid, woman, it is me.)

The two women went into the house and Khethang went back to his sleep.

''M'akena, *mosali oa Molimo, ho etsahalang keng?'* (Woman of God, what is happening?) 'M'atsepo inquired with utter amazement.

Aunt tried to relate her sad story, but she could not finish her sentences, because she was shivering all over.

'Give me a blanket, my friend, I am dying of cold,' 'M'akena pleaded.

'M'atsepo, who was disoriented because of the hour and the shock of her friend's condition, had not realised that her friend was terribly cold until then, so she lit the paraffin heater and gave aunt a blanket. Aunt then related the story of how she was chucked out of her house. At the end of her narration, she asked, ''M'atsepo, *ngoan'eso,* (my dear) what must I do? Please help me. My life with *Ntate* Thabo is as hostile as that of a cat and mouse. Ah, this marriage. I am scared of it!'

'*Mosali*, true enough we are God-fearing women, but this is beyond our control. I advise you to sue this man. How can you live with a monster in the house?' 'M'atsepo asked. However, the two women knelt down and prayed:

Our Father who are in Heaven,
Hallowed be thy name, thy will be done,
In earth as it is done in Heaven.
Lord, we need your guidance
in this particular matter.
O! Merciful God, please show us the way.
Lord, our God, remember you said that
We should cast all our burdens unto
You, for you care for us. Again Lord
You said you would never let the righteous
Suffer. Why then, Lord, do you let us suffer?
But finally, Lord, I want to acknowledge
Your power and lordship. There is none
Like you. I want to thank you for
Watching over my soul.
May your name be glorified,
In Jesus' name I pray,
       Amen.

After this prayer 'M'e 'M'akena mastered some courage, and she could feel more hope and enthusiasm in her veins. The two women realised that they were mistaken to seek to sue *Ntate* Thabo. Rather, what came to their minds were the Biblical words, 'Vengeance is mine, thus says the Lord.' Aunt made the decision to remain.

Breaking the train of her story, aunt spoke directly to me: 'Setho, my child, anchor your faith in the Lord, for He never fails anyone.'

Then aunt continued her story, telling me that three days after her dispute with *Ntate* Thabo, he was struck by a heart attack, so that he had to be hospitalized for three months. On discharge, he was warned that his life was at stake, and he should abstain from alcohol. He was also cautioned that he should not get angry, as that could cause his death.

The face of my aunt was beaming as she concluded the sad side of the story of her life with *Ntate* Thabo.

'Glory to God, His ways are beyond our understanding and His thoughts are unsearchable!' she declared.

'What do you mean?' I asked.

'From that moment on, there emerged remarkable peace in my family, so much that everybody in the village of Tsoelike was shocked because of the joy and happiness which governed my family. My child, this was the turning point of my sorrowful life. *Ntate* Thabo now became a loving and supportive father to his family.'

It was during this peaceful period in their marriage that *Ntate* Thabo got a stroke of good luck and was employed as a messenger at the Mpiti Local Court. One day, when overwhelmed with gratitude for his good fortune, Ntate Thabo said to his wife: *''M'akena mosali oa khomo tsa ntate, mosali oa Bakoena, ha ke tsebe hore na nka u etsetsang? Ha ke so bone mosali ea bohale, ea mamello joalo ka uena tjena. Ke lekile ha ngata ho u hlorisa ka sehloho empa oa nna oa ntlhompha, oa mpontsa lerato, oa ikokobetsa.'* (Makena, the wife of my father's cattle, the daughter of the Bakoena clan, I don't know what I can do for you. I have never seen a woman who is so wise and tolerant as you. I have tried several times to persecute you, but you kept on respecting me, showing me love, and you humbled yourself.)

My aunt and uncle lived together harmoniously for more than two years, but sad news came one day in January 1967. Their son, Moeketsi, who was staying with his uncle Sekhonyana at Mosenekeng, had been struck dead by lightning while tending his uncle's flock.

When the news reached him, *Ntate* Thabo cried out, 'Oh! My God, what do I hear? This can't be true,' and he collapsed in a faint.

Moeketsi was their youngest son, and as in most families, he was the most loved. Indeed he was the child at the heart of his parents. *Ntate* Thabo had to be rushed to the hospital, and within two weeks, he too had ceased breathing.

The Universe

'MASEFINELA MPHUTHING

Behold the beauty of the universe, as the mother earth
    starts adorning herself with a green magnificent
    robe on a brown 'wet-look' body after the
        passage of the torrential rains.

As the cheerful springtime commences knocking on
    the door of the melancholy winter announcing
    her turn of office;

In accompaniment, the lilies and gladioli come
    quivering and shivering to the tune of
    a sweet music, spreading their wings wide
    on the waves of the cool breeze;
        the sweet fragrance is carried, traversing
        the valleys dotted with welcoming lilies,
        the valleys' waters enfold and ripple in
        obedience to the instruction of the
            howling winds;

The wind chases the softspoken breeze,
    the imposing and domineering wind
    now its high pitched voice and
    whistles are heard echoing
        in the mimicking caves and mountains.

The dusk approaches, the sun prepares herself for
    a repose, for the Goddess of Sleep awaits
    fatigued and harassed workers.

One, two, three stars start peeping shyly on the
deep blue royal sky, signifying 'l'avenir'
of the Queen of Heaven, the Moon;
    she is the chaperon of lovers,
    the guardian of shepherds.
        Magically does she anoint the
        green robe with a glittering oil.
        Oh! what an epochal chase!

Why Blame Her?

'M'ATSELENG LENTSOENYANE

'M'athato's husband was over-possessive. He roamed about like a he-goat in summer, but he would not hear of her visiting friends. He argued that a woman is a hen; she has to stay at home as fowls are kept in a fowl-run. But a man is a turkey which goes out to the veld hunting for insects. To him, for a woman to visit friends was to expose herself to other men.

Sometimes he locked her in the house overnight and went – where? She did not know. But on the day she decided to quit, he was a fierce animal. A lion. It was Sunday afternoon, and he had been away the whole morning. When he came back, he claimed that he was tired. He said that if he had a child, he would have sent it on his errands.

Before 'M'athato could even respond, there came a knock at the door. A boy of about six years of age entered. He reported that his suckling sister was ill, and so his mother was asking for money. To 'M'athato's surprise, Thabiso asked for that day's collection, whether the taximan had left it. 'M'athato nodded her head and pointed at the drawer where the money was usually kept. She sweated from anger. Thabiso took out the whole bundle and went out, the boy following him.

When he came back he did not return the remaining money to its usual place. Instead he pushed it inside his back pocket. 'M'athato asked, '*Ntate*, what's happening? Whose child is that boy, and why does his mother report this to you?'

Thabiso shook his head and said, 'I am sorry, that concerns me and me alone. Anyway, when my child is ill I have to know.'

'Your child!' burst out the angry 'M'athato with a shaky voice.

According to traditional Basotho practice, when a family is childless, it negotiates marriage for the husband to a second wife, whose work is to bear children for the first one. The children are raised according to the first wife's likings. But some men choose to roam about with concubines to avoid paying direct support for the children. Thabiso decided to go about with concubines, in part to hurt his childless wife.

'Ah! But how can you do this? How can you – ?' 'M'athato did not finish her sentence because Thabiso interrupted her.

'Where is your child? Do you think I am so blind that I do not see what you have done? You will know me. Do you remember what that traditional doctor said?' he shouted angrily.

'But how can you believe all that he said? Why do you refuse to allow me to go to the specialists on women's sicknesses?' 'M'athato questioned.

Thabiso did not allow her to go to the clinic because he feared that she would be operated on to prevent child-bearing. His face suddenly changed; it became as black as a three-legged pot, while his eyes glittered like those of a poisonous snake. He slapped her across her face with the back of his hand, locked the door, and fetched out his *kubu*. He whipped, kicked and tossed her, not caring about the furniture on which she fell.

As she related these events to her visitors, 'M'athato took off her headcloth to show them the shaved patches and a two-stitched wound above her right eye. She sighed and said, 'My husband was not a person, but a cannibal, a bloodthirsty man-eater. He used anything he came across to beat, no, to kill me. He roared, insulted and called me a bull.'

'*Ao! Batho!*' 'M'ampho, 'M'athuso and I exclaimed, all three. We had heard 'M'athato was staying with her sister. She, like us, was a member of the Women's League, which devotes itself to the church and to consoling its members who suffer physically and spiritually and need prayers. The League had sent us to meet our equal and to see what we could do for her.

'A bull!' we cringed. This phrase is commonly used by husbands and mothers-in-law to abuse or ridicule barren women.

'M'athato continued, 'His eyes reddened like those of a wild cat chasing chickens in their fowl-run. I had never seen him like that.' Tears welled inside her eyes and she stopped.

'But how did you escape death?' I asked.

'God was with me. I hit through the window-pane with my forehead and forced myself out. He chopped my back with his panga or something like a sharp butcher-knife as I passed through. This wound is from the window,' she replied, pointing at her forehead. 'I have never gone back to him except when I was escorted by a policeman to fetch my clothes and documents.'

We knew the background of 'M'athato's story. Three years after her marriage she had joined the League. She used to report her clashes with her husband, and we had prayed with her often.

Traditionally, *ngoetsi* is expected to conceive as early as two months after her arrival in her husband's family, or at least within the first year. If she doesn't fall pregnant within that expected time, she is taken to the traditional doctors who check to see whether she is free from disease or witchery. So, after a year, 'M'athato was taken to the family traditional doctor.

She was given *litaola* on which she sprinkled her saliva, and then she threw them over a goat-skin used specifically for that purpose. The doctor unfolded that she was bewitched but said that was a small matter if she promised to follow the precautions. 'M'athato, who was desperately in need of a child, confirmed that even if she had to pass through water or fire, as long as she could become a real mother, she would gladly do so. She was given many bundles of herbs and powdered substances to be consumed or used in a bath.

All the directions she followed until she had finished all the bitter and bad-smelling herbs. She waited hopefully to see changes, but none came. Her husband's love deteriorated, and he suspected that she had not used the medicines. His age-mates began being called after their children: Rathabo, Ramoliehi.* Thabiso became embittered because he had no new name. He began to call 'M'athato names and ceased his usual jokes. He brought no more presents to her. He was not prepared to share the problem with his wife. He started to have secret outings with other women and to come home late.

In 1979, Thabiso's last-born sister came to stay with them. She

---

* Ra- means father of: Rathabo means father of Thabo, Ramoliehi is father of Moliehi; the Ra- is given to the man after his child's naming.

was being kept away from *chobeliso*. 'M'athato at least had company: someone to talk to; someone to reduce her boredom, someone with whom to while away some time. But 'M'athato was still worried and frustrated by her husband's absences: maybe he has fallen into robbers or thieves who have killed him after picking his pockets, she thought. Or he can be killed by other men over lovers.

Sometimes he arrived so late that 'M'athato was asleep already and he woke her up to prepare his supper if it could still be called so. To get up, especially on winter nights, was a real sacrifice for 'M'athato. So she would sometimes serve his dinner and cover it up on the table for him to eat whenever he came home. He would wake her up and complain that he could not eat ice-cold food.

When 'M'athato asked him where he had been, he would say that a man is never asked such a question because he is a bull of all kraals , and he is a security-guard by himself. He emphasized that a woman is a child; she has no right to tell her husband what to do or not to do. Hers is to supply the man with what he wants.

'M'athato told Thabiso's sister that she was worried about Thabiso's outings, especially when they stretched on past midnight. The sister tried to talk to him, but Thabiso rebuked her by saying that she was too young to be involved in such cases.

As she faced us, 'M'athato remembered many things. One day Thabiso found a man's boot print on the front steps. He locked the two women in the house and asked them who was the man they kept there when he was not at home. They answered that the boot print came from a passer-by who was asking for directions. Thabiso did not believe that. He whipped them both. They yelled, cried and shouted, but knowing him, no one came to rescue them.

In the morning 'M'athato's face was swollen and her lower teeth were loose. She could not chew, but had to swallow small bits of food and drops of liquid. Therefore she stole away to her family.

According to the custom, if a wife goes to her home after a family quarrel, her husband is expected to go and ask her to come back. His main purpose is to show respect to his wife's family. As the family settles the dispute, he has to apologize and show his deep repentance. After a month or so, Thabiso, accompanied by his uncle, went to his wife's family.

After a long, serious talk, Thabiso apologized and asked for his wife to return to their home. The parents made an excuse that she had to go for a medical check-up first; it was only after that that she could go back to him. That was a polite way of saying we have to follow customary practice. When she goes back to her home, she has to carry along a sheep's head and some pieces of the mutton, so her parents had to provide it. That is a sign that the family has forgiven the son-in-law, and it expects him not to hit her again. If she does not bring that share of a sheep, she will be ridiculed. People will say she has brought a black sheep's head. It is a disgrace to the woman. So when her family was able to provide the sheep's head, she went home.

Thabiso had not changed, however. The only time 'M'athato and Thabiso stayed together peacefully was Christmas Day. Thabiso likes roasted meat, so every Christmas he would slaughter a sheep. Each time visitors would arrive, he would make up fire and roast some. 'M'athato would bring soft drinks or *motoho*. Then the family would rejoice.

But unfortunately on Christmas Day 1981 'M'athato's cousin arrived. 'M'athato brought out her album to show her cousin all her recent photos. 'M'athato was shocked when she found a snapshot of a six-month-old baby whom she didn't know. It became an embarrassment when the cousin asked about the photo and 'M'athato could only say it was her first time to see it. Thabiso said nothing.

'M'athato would never scold her husband in public. She would suppress her anger until nightfall and complain to him only when they were in bed, so that no third party overheard their quarrel. That night 'M'athato inquired about the photo.

'*Ntate*, whose photo is that in the album?'

'It is my baby's photo, but why do you want to poke your nose in my private affairs? Never ask me anything about that photo again,' Thabiso answered angrily.

'What! Poke my nose! But I found the photo inside my album.

Whose privacy is that?' He made no answer. She paused, regained her composure, and continued, '*Ntate*, why can't you arrange to marry a second wife, since you want a child so much? Let me go back to my parents. I will be pleased to. For you know, as a Christian, I cannot stay in a polygamous family.'

'I can't marry a second wife. That would be jumping from a frying pan straight into the fire. I would have to keep you both, and I know that women are weaker vessels. They cannot tolerate each other. I would have to settle quarrels all the time, sometimes with a whip. It would be twice the headache I have now.'

'But the kind of life we are leading now is unhealthy. I fear for your security as you go from place to place at night. Your enemies may be after your every step. More than that, what about our everyday clashes? Don't you think this can be solved in one way or another?'

'I don't want to crack my head with a second wife. I know that I have children. When I want to look at a baby, the photo will do. You know very well that a child is its parents' image and dignity. But you, I cannot tolerate to miss. You are my father's cattle wife. My ancestors forbid.'

'M'ampho asked 'M'athato when Thabiso's beatings and tortures became intolerable. 'M'athato recalled that 1984 began as a bright or different year. Thabiso got a taxi, and they ran it together. Every day's collection was recorded inside 'M'athato's bank account book, while Thabiso kept the book. The business flourished and their life changed to an easy, co-operative one.

But 'M'athato explained, 'Whenever there is peace in the family, onlookers become jealous. They told stories to my husband about me.'

We nodded.

'All of a sudden Thabiso changed; he started to pinpoint minute mistakes and to abuse me: I am careless, I don't know how to cook. Sometimes he went to the extent of saying I smell bad, which implied that I used witchcraft charms to attract him. Thabiso refused to eat my food.'

With difficulty, 'M'athato continued, 'Once again Thabiso went back to his concubines. He spent days away, or nights. He forced me to withdraw all the money from our joint account at the bank.

He opened his own account. I did not know the taxi collections anymore. I had no money. He would go shopping and supply only groceries. I sought advice from his uncle, who tried to talk with us.

Uncle took us to Dr Ramatlapeng, who found that it is impossible for me to conceive because some delicate female parts are injured. I recalled that I once fell from a bicycle when I was doing my primary education. Maybe that was the cause. I am sure this medical evaluation was the final cause of Thabiso's frustration. The intrusion of the boy asking for money for his suckling sister was only the spark of fire which fuelled the anger inside Thabiso.

'But then, has he come to see you, or fetch you back home?' I asked.

'No, he hasn't, but rumours say that he is proudly announcing that he knows that I will go back because his father's spirit will haunt me if I don't,' 'M'athato grinned.

'So what is your reaction to that remark?' asked 'M'athuso, very concerned.

'Nothing will force me to go back except to wear his mourning cloth if he can die before me,' 'M'athato answered firmly.

The African Goddess
The Figure in My Past

MONICA NTHABELENG RAMAROTHOLE

'Strike me dead, Nthabeleng my friend, if you find me getting married to a Mosotho man!' Thandeka declared as she lay on the bed next to Nthabeleng's.

The two room-mates had just finished high school and were preparing for their final exams. They felt their time together was drawing to a close, and they had begun telling each other their life stories and secrets. Thandi's South African background often led her to disapprove of the customs which had marked (and often hampered) Nthabeleng's progress toward womanhood. They were discussing names. Nthabie said, 'I prefer being called Monica. My Sesotho name always reminds me of my past.'

'But Monica isn't an African name. It's a colonial hangover,' Thandi argued, 'while Nthabeleng is such a nice name! It means "Rejoice with me", right?'

'Yes. But you don't know how I got it.'

'How, then?'

'As far as I can remember, my mother has always been working for a white couple in Johannesburg; so obviously she's a stranger to me. Unlike your mother, my mom spent the whole year away from us, and she came home only for Christmas.

'I grew up in my grandmother's family without a name and without identity or self-esteem. Some people called me Simeme; others called me 'Meimeng, depending on which one they felt comfortable with. They wanted to conceal my present name, which you're so fond of, because they said it contaminated their clan.'

'Hae! hae!' Thandeka exclaimed, 'This is ridiculous and absurd. How could they say such a thing?'

'I hope you are going to listen. The problem was that my grandmother asserted that I was not her son's daughter. She argued that since she did not know me, I was not going to have the names from the Bakoena, as I might have descended from other clans. In this country, the Bakoena are the only people to reckon with, because the King belongs to their clan.'

'I also have a feeling that they think they are as pure as the Virgin Mary and her son Jesus Christ,' said Thandeka with disgust.

'Exactly! My grandmother was like that. From the time I was four to seven years old, I lived in her home and for that whole period I was heavily abused: my grandmother punished, insulted me and condemned me. She got angry at everything I did until such time as I could not distinguish right from wrong.'

'How can a woman do such things to an innocent child? Nthabeleng, are you sure that you are telling the truth?'

Nthabeleng continued her story as if she did not hear her friend's remark. Her face seemed darker, and her eyes were fixed on the opposite wall above Thandeka's head.

'In my culture, children are always told that God is the provider of children. It is said that when a woman wants a child, God directs her towards a nearby dam or river, where a huge water-animal emerges and gives the baby to her. With this kind of illusion, the young ones survive, shut off from the realities of the adult world.

'But as for me, my grandmother proclaimed to the public that one day she would take me back to the man who bore me. I misconstrued this man she was always telling me about to be God, the provider of children. At Sunday School, I was told that God is the father of everybody, and so I thought He was the one who bore me. One day, I even shouted at my grandmother that she must take me there at once, because daily insinuations had got into my nerves, and it was worse than Hell!'

'Hm! Nthabeleng, you must have cursed that woman to her grave. *Kannete!* She deserved it.' Thandeka retorted with a sharp voice.

'Thandi, *Ngoan'eso*,' Nthabie sighed, 'that woman is still alive to see to my fate. To her I was always the black sheep. I survived in a whirl of emotional struggle without anybody's help. Even the villagers could not understand, because they failed to see that my grandmother's hand became harder whenever she confronted me. I was going to get a beating no matter what I did, so there was no point in trying to please her.

'As a result, I did everything whenever I wanted and nobody could force me into anything. Many times she would order me to do a certain household duty, and I would tell her to leave that to the children she knew. "My unknown father," I yelled at her, "is the only one in this world who can give me orders."

'The old woman taught me all that went with brutality, and I proved to be very severe in employing such tactics. Every day, I got out of bed with an agenda: to humiliate her. I thought of nothing but strategies for disgracing my grandmother.

'One day I got sick. Because I was often sullen, withdrawn and very shy, people realized late that I was indeed in trouble. It came as a common cold, developed into an overwhelming fever, and culminated in chicken-pox. It was only when the traces of chicken-pox appeared on my body that my grandmother began to pay a certain degree of attention to me. She brought traditional herbs from the nearby mountains and asked my eldest brother to smear them all over my body. She boiled some of these herbs and gave me to drink, but I refused. They would force the bitter liquid into my mouth until I would vomit. My body's temperature increased daily, and I spent sleepless nights. I became very weak, as I could not eat anything, and my eyes looked like bore-holes.'

'Your grandmother must be a witch, Nthabeleng, my friend. I don't understand her behaviour,' Thandeka said with sympathy as she watched Nthabeleng grow pale with grief.

Nthabeleng continued, 'My grandmother refused to take me to the hospital, arguing that she did not have money. I bet she wanted me to die right where I was lying. But I had a strong desire to survive and get revenge.

'One night, my sickness overpowered my body so much that I could not speak, see, or hear anything from anybody. They paid very little attention to this, as they thought I was only being stubborn. I felt terribly exhausted, and in the end, I cannot tell what happened. The next day when I woke up, it was very late in the afternoon and I sort of heard some buzzing sounds which I thought came from a distance. I tried to listen, but a sharp pain struck my brain, and I fell into an unusual sleep. After some time, I woke up again. There were some people singing in the hut. They were many; I don't remember how many.

'They were singing; I was listening. Not because I understood their song, but because that was the only thing in my power to do. I tried to think about where I was, but my head refused me. I wanted to scratch my tingling body; my hands refused to move. I was tired and feeling a terrible pain all over my body.

'I looked at each person around me and read from their faces an element of hypocrisy. I wondered at the presence of the priest in their midst and could not figure out why he was there. My elder sister was with them, crying. My eldest brother seemed to brood over something; and my grandmother was singing with complete indifference.

'They stopped the song, and it was at this time that I realized that they had been singing a hymn. The priest came over to my mat, and at this moment I thought I knew what was happening: they thought I was going to die, and so they fetched the priest. The reverend gentleman was here to pray for me so that I might be received with ceremonial spirit into the heavenly kingdom.

'As he was reciting his prayer with his hands raised high over my swollen body, I wondered if I was being given as a sacrifice for the Lord. I was aware that everybody was there because of me. As the priest mounted his divine abstract statements, some of which he quoted from the Bible, I looked at my poor body already covered with sores and ring-worms. I remembered the biblical Job. I looked at the blankets with which I was half covered – they were dirty. I longed for a cleaner place. I wanted to get up there and then, and leave for my mother's place. But Ha Likupa was too far for a young sick girl of six to get to, alone. Besides, I did not have money and then, the place was empty.

'It was extremely quiet in the hut, and the voice of the priest was vivid. I got the power to stand up from the mat and struggled for balance. The priest continued to pray for me, and since his eyes were closed, he did not see that I had got up from my death mat and was watching him with burning curiosity.

'I swore to myself that I must live to disgrace my grandmother and all her friends in that hut. I wanted to show her that if she thinks she is an African goddess, to me, she is not. I would live regardless of her hatred for me. I wondered whether the priest's God would hear his prayers. I remembered many times I had called to my God to help me out of my grandmother's cruel thrashings and could not get any answer. The more I called to Him, the more she beat me, and so I swore from my insides that I hated his God as well as my grandmother's.

'Ultimately, the word "Amen," was spoken and everybody looked at me with amazed eyes. My elder sister smiled at me to express her gratefulness, and my brother gasped in disbelief. The priest tried to touch me on my shoulder, but I retreated.

'Don't be afraid, child, I want to help you,' he assured me.

'He approached me again and I spat at his feet and rushed for the door. My grandmother grabbed me and cursed me for degrading her holy man, and I spat on her face. She tried to slap me across the face but my brother got hold of her hand. I reached for the doorway and turned to give her my last word: "Don't dare touch me, you old witch, or else you are going to fly through that little window of yours!" I shouted angrily and rushed for the gate.

'However I was very weak. My feet refused to carry me any further. I stumbled over my own imbalance: darkness overcame me.

'When I regained consciousness, I was lying in hospital. My lovely aunt was sitting on my pillow, holding her rosary high and pleading to the God of the Catholics to let me live. She is the youngest sister in my mother's family. She told me about how she found me half-dead in my grandmother's hut and rushed me to the hospital. She had been praying for me ever since I came into the hospital.

'My aunt was convinced that the old woman hated me so much that she would even make merry over my dead body. She could not understand why I was not taken to the hospital under such conditions. Consequently, she swore that I would never set foot in my grandmother's home again.

'Indeed I never went there again. I promised my aunt that I would live to retaliate. The old woman needs to see me going up the ladder while she is swimming in the mud of poverty.' Nthabeleng sighed very deeply and continued, 'My friend, this is what has been motivating me right from primary up through high school. Each time I remember my grandmother – the African goddess without a sin – I make sure that I am well up-to-date with my studies. I want to pass my examinations so that I will be able to be admitted into the university. I want to show my grandmother that she is not the Lord who "is a jealous God, visiting the iniquity of the 'mothers' upon the children into the third and fourth generation of them that hate God."'*

Nthabeleng's eyes met Thandi's, and the two girls giggled together sleepily.

* Exodus 20:5.

What about the Lobola?

ANONYMOUS

Translated by CLEMENT MOIKETSI MATJELO

In 1979 I first began to develop nascent feelings for the vocation. I was a devout Catholic, and my family was also Catholic. The year before, the first nuns had arrived in our village, and they stayed at the Catholic Church. It was a turning point in my life.

I was then already an adolescent girl of nineteen. I had many boyfriends, and there were those I loved very much, but Joe was my favourite. He was by all standards a handsome young man, and every girl in our village was nuts about him. But then I had won Joe and the other girls envied me.

The arrival of the nuns changed all this. I was fascinated by their dress and their way of life, but mostly I felt preoccupied by their benevolent deeds. Sometimes they would go around the village visiting old people; they would pray for them and sometimes offer them material assistance such as clothing, although most of the clothes were reach-me-downs. Very soon I became absorbed with thoughts about these nuns.

'Were they ordinary human beings, or perhaps angels just descended from heaven?' I wondered. Really, I felt I wanted to be like them so much that I would forego all my pleasures, and I would even part with Joe, if I could only be like these holy creations!

One evening when no one was around except my mother and I, I took courage and talked to her about these nuns: *'M'e,* aren't these nuns very nice people?' I asked her. She looked at me cynically for a moment and then replied: 'Yes, my daughter, they are nice people; but don't tell me you also want to be a nun!'

I stood confused for a moment and then said,

'But why, *'M'e?'* My mother looked angry and disappointed.

'You know, Palesa, I personally bear no hard feelings against nuns. God knows! It's just that your father dislikes them. Your father and I nearly divorced a few years back because your sister said she wanted to join the sisterhood, and I supported her.' My mother paused.

'So that's why you weren't on speaking terms for a while?' I asked her. But she was uncomfortable and seemed to want to dismiss the issue.

'Yes, Palesa, that's why. But please, let's not talk about this any more; and make sure you never mention this in your father's presence. I'm afraid this time it could lead to a real divorce. So go now and prepare the supper.'

As I was preparing our meal, I remembered that my mother never missed a single church service. Even when she was sick, she would just drag her weak body to the church. I recalled the day when dad beat her for persisting in going to church in spite of the fact that she had been seriously ill the previous day. That Sunday morning, the rain was pouring down in torrents. While mother was busy making her preparations for church, dad was watching her from the corner of his eye, as though he would suddenly pounce on her like a lion. He did not utter a word.

When she had finished preparing herself, *'M'e* strapped me on her back, since I was then a little girl of four, and she took her Bible to leave for church. She had hardly made two steps away from the door, when suddenly I felt my forehead splashing into the mud, and after that all I could hear were pathetic screams for help from my mother. My father was hitting her all over the body with a heavy stick like the ones used by shepherds to beat cattle. I was too mesmerized to cry. My elder brother, who was afraid to intervene, snatched me from the muddy ground and darted into the house carrying me in his arms. Outside there were already voices from neighbours pleading to my father to stop. When he did stop, he went into the bedroom and locked himself inside. One of the neighbours, *Ntate* Mohau, brought his van, and my mother was rushed to hospital.

Sitting alone in the kitchen, my thoughts shifted to the nuns at church. I tried very hard to keep these thoughts out of my mind, but it was to no avail. I did not want to disappoint my father by retaining my ideas about the sisterhood, but the temptation was insurmountable.

'I must go and see my sister,' I thought to myself. 'Perhaps she can tell me what to do.'

The fact was that my sister, after giving up her desire to join a nunnery, since our father was adamantly against that decision, had eloped with her boyfriend who lived at the nearby village. I wanted to see her. When I told my mother of my plan to visit my sister 'M'atlala, *'M'e* did not inquire much about it; just asked me not to stay too long lest I outstay my welcome.

Ever since she had eloped, 'M'atlala was a very unhappy woman. She often came to *'M'e* to tell her how she lived with a brute of a man who beat her day in and day out. What moved me most in her accounts was when she reminded *'M'e* of how she had loved the sisterhood but *'M'e* and *Ntate* had prevented her from joining. She was now bound to live with the brute for the rest of her life, she would say, bursting into tears. *'M'e* would be very hurt by this and would defend herself by arguing that it was our father who insisted that he wanted *lobola* like other men whose daughters were married.

When I arrived at my sister's place, she was sitting outside under a peach tree, suckling her third child. Already, at the age of twenty-five, she looked like a haggard crone. I swore to myself that I would never be married. I would never, never get married to any man! After we had exchanged greetings and she had served me with some porridge to eat, she said to me: 'But you look troubled, Palesa. What's the matter?'

Instead of answering her, I was embarrassed and pondered for a moment. I wondered, 'Have I advertised my problems on my forehead?' Finally I got up the courage to speak.

'You're right, *Ausi* 'M'atlala. The trouble is, I want to join the sisterhood.'

'What? Have I heard you well?' 'M'atlala asked, surprised but also obviously pleased. 'Look here, Palesa, *Ntate* will twist your neck if he hears this. Do you know that?'

Instead of responding to her, I burst into tears and kept on crying, 'I want to be a nun. A nun.'

My sister patted me on the shoulder. In a low tone she said to me, 'Truly speaking, I also love the sisterhood. It's just that my plans were frustrated by *Ntate*. But don't worry, I know what we should do. I will help you,' she said reflectively.

Was I dreaming? Did my sister say she knows what to do? I wondered. 'That would be a breakthrough! My father can't stop me now,' I caught myself saying aloud. The determination was there in me, and it was building every moment.

My sister told me that she was friends with one of the sisters at the convent in the village. She would arrange with the sister that I should pay regular visits to the convent so that I could see their life before deciding to join the sisterhood. Luckily, the sister was very happy to hear about my plan, and she agreed with my sister that I should pay them visits during my stay there.

Everything went smoothly, and I was overjoyed to visit the convent. I could tell you about the many things I observed during my visits there, but then I am not supposed to. Let me only tell you that I deeply fell in love with everything I saw there, so much that after only two visits I had made up my mind to join. But then, the problem was that all aspirants to the sisterhood were supposed to obtain parental permission before they could be admitted. I knew that my mother would support me, but then, my father . . . he was just a stone-hearted lion!

It was about a month since I left home to visit 'M'atlala, and I was sure that *'M'e* must be getting impatient and upset by my long absence. Indeed, one morning my sister received a letter from her. She had told *Ntate* about my plan, and he was fuming and no longer talked to her. As she wrote that letter, she said, all the relatives had been called to come and deliberate on my behaviour. I was to return immediately.

That night, my sister and I did not sleep at all. She spent the whole night briefing me on what to say in front of the elders. She told me to check my words so that I would not infuriate *Ntate*, because he would twist my neck until my poor soul left its body. To make sure that I would not forget what she told me, she wrote all the points down for me on a piece of paper so that I could revise them when I got back home.

Uncle Oupa lived twelve miles away from our home town, in a

village called Ha Mpiti. Ever since my childhood, I was very fond of him, and indeed, he called me his 'favourite daughter'. Hardly two months passed without my visiting his family. If I did not show up, he would send his eldest daughter, 'M'amkhize, to fetch me. Uncle Oupa provided all the security, love and comfort which I lacked from my father. By vocation, he was an Archbishop of the Apostolic Churches in our region. All our relatives were proud of him. I suppose he understood me because, more than any of his children, I loved going to church.

The idea of returning home terrified me. How could I possibly face the elders and be able to answer their reproachful questions? When I thought of my father, I nearly pissed my panties. He was just a lion, a lion, you know! I prayed that Uncle Oupa would be there among the elders, because perhaps he would come to my rescue. But how could I know his stand on the matter? He might be even more antagonistic than anyone else. Oh! how ashamed would I be to disappoint Uncle Oupa.

As this train of thoughts passed through my mind, the bus was getting nearer and nearer my home. At last when the bus arrived at the gate, I nearly fainted when I saw my father standing outside watching me. He looked as black as a pot that had never known any washing since it came from the shop. When I was about to greet him, his voice cracked out at me, as though it had long been sealed in an airtight bottle: 'Is this the time a girl should arrive home, Palesa, hm? Tell me!' Instead of answering him, I only broke into tears and wailed as loudly as I could. That was only my arrival home. I still had to await the day of reckoning, when all the elders would be glaring at me. I felt like the earth would crack and swallow me.

That day of reckoning came without refusing. In the morning, I woke up with my eyes swollen like scones as a result of too much crying the previous night. By 8 a.m., the elders were already gathered outside and seated on stools which formed a circle. In the middle of that circle was a mat for me to sit on. My mother was seated on another mat outside the circle. When I saw that Uncle Oupa was seated among the elders, I was slightly encouraged. However, he wore such a pale look on his face that I was suddenly bereft of all hope.

My father roared, 'Come here, Palesa!' I felt as though his voice was cutting into my flesh like a sharp knife. I cannot tell you what happened after that, except from what my mother told me late that night.

She said that when *Ntate* called me, I screamed once and then fainted. Uncle Oupa was so furious that he slapped *Ntate* hard in the face. Then, like lightning, *Ntate* grasped Uncle's throat so hard that Uncle started to foam. Luckily, the other relatives intervened and separated them. Then it was suggested by one of the elders that the matter be dropped completely.

The following week my elder brother, who worked in the mines, arrived home. I was grateful when he arrived because I knew that he alone could approach *Ntate*. My father always respected him very much and heeded his advice. Like my mother and I, my brother was a devout church-goer and he was also pretty fond of the sisters. When I told him my problem, he said: 'According to our culture, I am your father, although *Ntate* is still alive. So I want to tell you that I release you with all my heart. There is nothing unusual about becoming a nun. The other sisters did not come from heaven; they were also human beings. If you ever come back, we will still accept you. There is nothing abnormal about coming back. If becoming a nun was a bad thing, I would be against it.'

I continued paying visits to the convent, and *Ntate* did not say anything. Finally I was told to come on 20 January 1980. When that day came, my mother called me into the kitchen to have a talk with me. She told me that the sisterhood was difficult, and she implored me that I should not disappoint her and my brother. Then she asked me if I had divorced all my boyfriends. I was embarrassed, because I didn't know she knew that I had boyfriends.

She insisted that I should write them letters and divorce them all before joining the sisterhood. I promised her that I would do as she requested, and I did divorce them, but also I explained to them that it was necessary because I was going to become a nun.

Then my mother and brother accompanied me to the convent, and we were heartily welcomed by the sisters. There were other newcomers like me, and they were also accompanied by their families. At lunch time we feasted around a large table covered with a white cloth. When the lunch was over, one of the sisters stood up and encouraged our parents that everything would be well with us.

At the convent, we were allowed to stay for two years before joining, and meanwhile we still attended ordinary school. When the two years had elapsed, we were taken to the Novitiate where we were going to learn about being nuns. After our studies at the Novitiate, we took our first vows, and it was only then that *Ntate* knew that I had joined the sisterhood. To my surprise, he gave me his consent. He even said that if my younger sister also wanted to join the sisterhood, he would allow her.

After the first vows, I took my second vows, which are the vows for life. Then to my amusement, every time I went home wearing my veil, *Ntate* seemed to be afraid of me. He would be the first one to order a hen to be slaughtered for me. Sometimes he would slaughter it himself. Then he would make me sit by his side, and he would ask me questions about the sisterhood. He was a transformed man; and I was a transformed woman.

Escape to Manzini

NOMAKHOSI MNTUYEDWA

The mist lifted slowly, and the naked plain boldly stared at us. We had crossed the border into Swaziland. We could have sighed with relief, yet we did not. We were tense with anxiety and fatigue. The journey between the Rand and Piet Retief had mostly been on a gravelled road in a middle-aged 'combi' that did not take the bumps with aplomb. We did not know what lay ahead, but we did know that there were border patrols. Policemen, European and non-European, slinging rifles and leading Alsatians. There could also be the odd mean Boer farmer who had taken it upon himself to trespass on Swaziland just to keep an eye on any *verdomde kaffir* daring to evade border controls.

A dog barked.

'*Yi ni leyo?*' (What is that?)

'*Yi nja.*' (A dog.)

'*I kuphi?*' (Where is it?)

'*Angazi.*' (I don't know.)

'*Sizo kwenzani manje?*' (What will we do now?)

'*Angazi.*' (I don't know.)

Our voices shook as we spoke. We snuggled the Woolworths shopping bags that we were using as travelling bags. Two for each one of us. We also carried plastic bags with 'provisions'. Mary had used all her remaining pennies, at least that is what she said, to provide me with *padkos*.

'*Ag man, moet jy vandag loop?*' (Oh man, must you leave today?)

'*Ja ma.*' (Yes ma.)

'*Hoekom?*' (Why?)

'*Die kar loop vandag.*' (The car leaves today.)

'*So?*'

'*Wat meen mama?*' (What do you mean, mama?)

'*So! Loop hierdie kar nie elke dag nie?*' (So! Does this car not leave every day?)

'*Nee. Een maal per week.*' (No. Only once a week.)

'*So! Moet jy hierdie week loop?*' (So! Must you leave this week?)

'*Skool begin môre.*' (School begins tomorrow.)

'*Hoekom het jy nie vir my gesê nie?*' (Why didn't you tell me?)

'*Jy het nie gevra nie.*' (You didn't ask.)

'*Ag man, nou moet ek my laaste pennies gebruik vir padkos en die fare.* (Oh, bother. Now I must use all my money for provisions and the fare.) We were alerted by a grind of gears that a vehicle of sorts was approaching us. It was coming from the South African side of the border. There was no place to hide. The alternative was to lie down flat in the veld and hope that our city clothes blended in well with the bush. Baba Mzimande had told us to dress plainly for the trip.

Baba Mzimande had made countless trips between Germiston and Swaziland, taking legal and illegal immigrants into the former protectorate. He changed entry points frequently to avoid detection. We heard of him through a friend of a friend, when Nolizwe and I voiced our concerns about Bantu education. We had heard that schools in the former protectorates were a lot better by comparison. We were also very tired of Soweto.

'*Le tsoa kae?*' (Where do you come from?)

'*Ha Hilda.*' (Hilda's place.)

'*Ha Hilda! Ha Hilda! Ha Hilda ke spoto! Leselenoa?*' (Hilda's! The shebeen! That drinking spa? Do you now drink?)

'*Mm-mmmh. Re ea tshaka.*' (We were only visiting.)

'*Letshakela Hilda oa le taoa? Bana ba banyane bakang lona!*' (You visit Hilda the drunkard? Young children like you!)

Voices raised in drunken argument. A flash of a knife. Blood. Screams. Confusion. Where will we go? What are we doing here? The police! Let's go. Run!

We catch the 4:30 a.m. train to Westgate. We have to be at the Commissioner's very early. Early bird, you know. At 10:30 we are still in line. The line does not seem to be moving. There are no benches. The door opens and closes. Someone goes out, but nobody goes in. It's tea-time, man. But how? The *ouens* have been in there all morning doing nothing, and now they are having a break. Lunch-time. Fish and chips do the rounds, and fat cakes. There's also syrupy Pepsi. You want 'Walls' or suckers? Have some.

After lunch there seems to be a slight improvement. More people are attended to. The *ouens* are over their *babalazi*. They've taken a couple at lunch-time. At 4:30 the doors close. Come back tomorrow. *Hau Bantu!*

The next day found us at Baba Mzimande's house.

'Ko-ko,' we knock.

'Ngena.' (Come in.)

'Nifunani?' (What do you want?)

'Ubab 'Mzimande.' (Mr Mzimande.)

'Ningobani Nina?' (Who are you?)

'I am Ndingu Nolizwe.

'Wena?' (And you?)

'Mna, Nosithukithezi.'

An agreement was reached very quickly. We were to be at his house on Tuesday night to leave for Swaziland.

An acrid smell curled up our nostrils all of a sudden. We were driving through the Usutu Forest, a manmade forest for the production of paper. It was nothing like the smell of overflowing nightsoil buckets, or the blocked or leaking sewage pipes that gave the Locations that inimitable smell, which was on occasion intermingled with the suffocating odour of coal or the pleasant smell of woodfires burning. And in summer, when the corn was ripe, the smell of the corn being braised over an open fire conjured up the comfortable feeling of a cramped home. There was also sometimes the smell of illegally brewed beer, Umqomboti. Those were the days before government won the battle and introduced beerhalls where Chibukussor 'shakeshake' was sold. And the smell of petrol fumes fused with all this. I liked all that air pollution. Maybe I was getting high on it.

As we drove through the green Swazi countryside, my mind flashed back to the first time I had been away from home. Park Station. Seated in a second class compartment, my sister and I were mildly apprehensive. The long overnight train ride from Johannesburg to Glencoe was to be an education, savvy though we were about the Johannesburg-Soweto line. We had been on it every day for three years, to go to school in Fordsburg, from Dube. Because third class was often stiflingly full, we had learned how to make ourselves comfortable in second, and when really daring, first class. Although the ticket examiners were vigilant, we succeeded more often than not in outsmarting them. Toilets were very good for hiding in. After all, how could an examiner flush anybody out of one? It was a delight to see the same tactics being used on the night train to Pietermaritzburg, and fine tuned to a Q.

'Ticket.'

'*Phuma wena! Phangisa.*' (Out you! Hurry.)

'*Usefikile. Ngena phantsi kwestulo wena. Phangisa man.*' (He has arrived. Under the bench. Quickly.)

'Ticket! Ticket!'

'*Hier is myne, baas.*' (Here is mine, boss.)

'*Hoeveel is julle?*' (How many of you are there?)

'Six.'

'*Ja. Julle is baie stout.*' (You are very naughty.)

'How, boss?'

'*Moenie cheeky wees!*' (Don't be cheeky!)

'*Ja baas.*'

Early morning. Wattle trees. A station in the middle of nowhere. Boisterous teenagers piling out of compartments. Some hungover. Dagga had been inhaled in large quantities and beer had coursed down many gullets. Mostly boys had indulged, but there had been a few girls. There had been a lot of vomiting.

A Bedford truck and several beat-up buses drove up to the platform and we all managed to squeeze ourselves, luggage and all, on to the vehicles. And there were black-habited nuns with white veils orchestrating everything, looking like penguins out of place in a tree-planted area.

'Ntombimbini, *kunuka ntoni?*' (What's smelling?)

'*Ngathi nga masimba e nkomo.*' (I think it's cow shit.)

'*Ubulongwe. Siphukuphuku.*' (Cow dung. Stupid.)

'How will we go to sleep?'

I fall asleep. The dormitory was hot and dark; it strongly smelled of cow dung which had been used to cement the floor and the inside of the wall. On the bunk beds were mattress covers. We were immediately instructed by Sister Margaret – tall, lean, stern and of rasping voice – to go outside where a pile of dry grass lay, and stuff the covers.

It was still dark outside when we were waked up by a deep toned hand bell. I did not recall ever having waked up that early, and for what? Prayers. My memories of that school are filled with heavy doses of prayer, porridge and more porridge, punctuated by a stew of samp and beans on Sundays; brown slices of bread and sweet black tea once a week – on Saturdays; sweets when there was a major Saint's Day celebration; shredded raw cabbage when we had scurvy; collecting wood from the forest twice a day; digging holes in the nearby forest to bury our excrement. When my mother met my sister and me at Park Station to welcome us back home for Christmas vacation, she cried. We did not go back.

Now here I was, on an interstate railway bus, to which I had transferred. Boys raucously paraded their sexuality in front of seemingly indifferent girls. Later, as we became experienced boarders, we got to know that from that indifference, rather complicated liaisons could develop, some leading to marriage.

A tall, plain-looking English nun met me on the veranda and greeted me kindly. 'You are?'

'Nolizwe.'

'Come into the office.'

Her sandalled feet led the way. I made it apparent I was an illegal immigrant. Sister Prudence did not seem perturbed by this news. I also told her that my mother knew that I had come to Swaziland, and would send school fees promptly as soon as she knew exactly where I was, and what was required of her. I was accepted at St. Michael's. I felt like a born-again Christian.

Ask Him to Explain

MPINE TENTE

When I was thirteen I left home in January for St. Agnes High School, some fifteen kilometres away. It was my first time away from my family, our two thatched rondavels and the chickens, dairy cattle and garden with which my parents supplemented their meagre incomes as school teachers. My grandmother rode with me on the bus and comforted me by gently holding my shaking hand.

As we alighted from the bus, it crossed my mind that both of us would need the other's assistance – my grandmother, Dondo, because of her old age; and me because I was scared out of my wits. Fortunately because of Dondo's seventy-plus years, two men helped us with the luggage: a medium-sized tin trunk containing blue school uniform, blankets, sheets, nighties and all the girls' essentials that were listed on my acceptance form. Nothing more, nothing less. The small provision trunk contained a roasted chicken, cakes and orange squash.

After introductions in the principal's office, Dondo informed the head teacher that she had my school fees and withdrew them from the neckline of her dress, where she had held them tightly to her breasts during the bus ride. It then dawned on me that I could not be trusted with anything. Handling the bus fare would have pushed me to the limits of my responsibility; school fees would be too much for a thirteen-year-old leaving home for the first time.

As the receipt for school fees was being signed and handed over to Granny, I knew the time to bid farewell to the last family member I still had with me was coming closer and closer. Tears rolled uncontrollably down my cheeks on to the new blue uniform dress with starched white collar and cuffs.

Dondo whispered that I should behave like a grown woman. Nobody was going to kill me. I watched her with sadness as she went back the same way we had come. I took a different direction in the company of three older girls.

This was a strange world, a world where people demanded an answer to every question, regardless of whether I felt the question personal or provocative. People feasted on one another's food without permission. And I was two days late, which made me the centre of attraction of both new and old students.

There was no one to hold my hand and comfort me. The only student I knew was Lineo, who had been my classmate and friend at primary school, but she was a 'day scholar'. That meant that at the end of the day she went back home and would return the following morning. I was on my own.

My heart beat faster than normal as I was approached by one of the senior girls. She asked me to follow her and informed me on our way to the dormitory that she was going to show me my kennel: which turned out to be my bed. The price I had to pay for my education included daily ridicule, making up other girls' beds, polishing their shoes, doing their washing, and receiving unnumbered beatings no matter how obedient I was.

I considered giving up and dreaded evenings especially, until a stroke of incredible good fortune turned me into an idol for a short while. One afternoon, during sports-time, new students were made to compete against each other in different track and field events. Our school was going to select a team to represent us in regional and national competitions. To my surprise, I was an excellent runner. I could not believe it was happening. There were cheers from all over the sports ground as I ran ahead of everyone and finished the race first.

There were suggestions that I should repeat the hundred-metre race with the school champ. She was in Form Three and had been the school idol for the past two years. I had never run competitively before. However that happened to be my day as I took the lead from the halfway mark to the finish line.

I surpassed my own expectations. I'd never had any idea that I was exceptional at anything. Most of my classmates came from well-known and well-to-do families. Some were chauffeured to and from school. Their parents were famous doctors, lawyers, senior government officials, and had important titles. Most of these titles were unfamiliar to this village girl who had climbed off the bus with her grandmother. But soon my name, Thato, became a household word. Both students and teachers came to know me as the fastest girl in the school, the School Champ. By March I was already selected for the school team and became the pride of the whole school. All selected athletes got special treatment – we were immediately put on a special diet.

The one-hundred-metre affair was my first success in life, and it gave me a taste of achievement which led to a desire to be ahead, do better and improve on what I had. The only area in which that did not prove useful was that of love relationships. I got off to a bad start, and my life right through university was punctuated with some disappointments and shattered dreams.

Before I went to high school, a love letter I wrote to a childhood sweetheart fell into the hands of one of my teachers. This teacher related the contents of the letter to my father, who was at the time a teacher in a senior grade at the same school. My father sent me home, where I was given a hiding and a serious warning against such 'bad' behaviour. As my father was beating me, I was pleading with my mother to ask for forgiveness on my behalf, a plea which fell on deaf ears. My father repeated, 'I won't let you disappoint me; I have such high hopes for your future.'

After the hiding, tears still rolling down my eyes, my body aching, I slowly walked the two hundred metres from my home to the school. Back in class, I could not work out the arithmetic exercise that was given to the class in my absence. A girl who sat next to me felt sorry for me and did the exercise for me. At that moment I made a commitment: no more love letters or intimate relationships with boys.

This commitment lasted until I was overcome by the temptation to experience the fantasies I heard about day in and day out from friends at St. Agnes. Girls talked about their exciting affairs, a subject which had been taboo to me. They were beginning to tease me because I had no such stories to tell, and they also questioned my womanhood.

I finally gave in to the advances of a boy from my class, Form

Three. Our affair was never as ideal and pleasant as the stories I used to hear. When I discovered that he was in love with another girl in the same school, I gave him an ultimatum: it was either me or the other girl. He failed to understand what the fuss was all about, and my ultimatum failed dismally.

This seemed to set a pattern which I continued weaving till I was grown. I tended to fall for already-sold property. That is, I always discovered later that whoever I was attracted to was 'legitimately' not mine. Even that childhood sweetheart had another girlfriend, my cousin. I spent my late teens wondering whether I was always second-best or whether I just never struggled enough to push everyone else out of the way.

Some friends of mine had a saying, '*monna ke qati oa lomisa-noa*', meaning one cannot have a man all to herself. Many seemed content with this idea and could not understand what I was complaining about.

'Isn't it fun to compete?' they would ask.

I had experienced the fun of competition on the track, but the idea of competing for the love of a man seemed remote to me. First of all, the rules of the game were never made clear. I could never understand what one needed to do in order to win. So after my second failure I decided to concentrate on other games whose rules were clear and easy to follow, games that might shape my future for the better.

In fact I had never seen a woman's ultimatum work. My mother never gave my father ultimatums; I never heard them argue, though I could see that my mother was not always happy with some of my father's decisions. I wondered whether reprimanding a man in our society was wrong. My friends told me to ignore and not question a man's behaviour; my mother never raised a finger to my father; my grandmother always warned me not to question my father. Dondo would repeatedly remind me of my father's sacrifices to send us through school and to clothe us, feed us and pay for our medication. Dondo and I mutually agreed on many issues, but we never saw eye to eye on one: men. She always cautioned me not to confront my male friends or to demand convincing answers from them.

'Man's behaviour,' she said, 'has since time immemorial been the way it is now. Difficult to understand, not easy to explain, and therefore not worth worrying about, because it cannot be changed.'

But I have always wanted to ask him to explain.

How I Became an Activist

HILDA 'M'AMAPELE CHAKELA

I found myself, at sixteen, in Form Two at a Roman Catholic high school in the district of Leribe. Given my background, I was trouble waiting for a place to happen. What surprises me now is how little trouble I caused for those nuns, and how much trouble they caused for me. We woke up at 5 a.m. and showered with cold water, whether it was winter or summer. In winter we dipped our face towels in the cold water and washed only our vital parts. We could not face this cold water. Then, after showers, we would walk in a line to the chapel, which was about a quarter of a mile from the dormitory.

The church was big, with a raised plank floor. Even now, when I hear the hollow echo of many feet on a plank floor, I get a cold shiver – the memory of all those mornings. All the girls sat on one side, with the reverend sister right at the back. Another sister would sit in the front. The boys from Sacred Heart used to come too. They would sit on the other side, with brothers watching over them at the front and the back.

The priest would come to celebrate the mass. Only Roman Catholics were allowed to receive holy communion, so of course I did not go. My South African mother had brought me up in the Anglican church. But I sang the hymns, trying to fit in and to please the nuns.

This was in the sixties, and great changes were taking place all over Africa. Talk of independence was everywhere. There was one man, a Mosotho (I will call him '*Ntate* Mookho', because he is still alive, although Mookho is not his real name) who was going around to all the Roman Catholic schools, telling the students lies about the Basutoland Congress Party and its leader, *Ntate* Mokhehle. Mokhehle was a Communist, according to Mookho, who claimed that *Ntate* Mokhehle was a fool to think the Basotho people could rule themselves. *Ntate* Mookho said the Basotho people were not capable of ruling themselves, because they were not as gifted as whites. *Ntate* Mookho addressed the whole student body in many schools and argued against home rule. He wanted the British to stay in Lesotho.

'Where would we get sugar,' he asked us, 'without the whites?' We could not make sugar for ourselves, apparently. 'Even clothing?' he asked. If we were left to ourselves, we were going to wear only little string skirts, the traditional *thethana*, not the western clothing we were wearing at our schools. He said that without the whites, we would be wearing animal skins instead of blankets. He told us that the reverend sisters and brothers and priests who came from Canada were so kind, because they had left great luxury in their countries; they left their wealth, and they dedicated their lives to us. They were living in this poverty-stricken Lesotho in order to educate us. We should be very grateful to them. Such talk sickened me.

He further said that if we got independence, *Ntate* Mokhehle would force the reverend sisters to marry him and the members of his party.

'*Ntate* Mokhehle is a Communist,' he raved. 'When he speaks, poisonous flames come out of his mouth.'

I had seen *Ntate* Mokhehle; he had visited my father's family. I knew he had no flames coming out of his mouth, and even less intention of marrying these Canadian nuns. So I used to ask this man questions. I would say, '*Ntate* Mookho, I know *Ntate* Mokhehle personally. I have attended B.C.P. meetings with members of my family. No one has ever said that they would force the sisters to marry them.'

My Uncle Charles Taolana Chakela was the treasurer of the B.C.P. I could not help arguing to put the record straight, but that really annoyed the white reverend sisters. I was labelled a cheeky, stubborn and argumentative child because I contradicted this wise man, Mookho, who was telling us what we needed to know for our own good. Here was a Mosotho, they said, one of us; if he did not know the truth about us, who did?

Many years later we learned that *Ntate* Mookho was paid by

the Roman Catholics to lecture to the children against independence and against Basotho politicians. He said that if independence had to come, we should support the Basutoland National
Party, the B.N.P., because they were Christians, not Commun-
ists like the B.C.P. The Roman Catholic children were told that I
was not like them; that I was dangerous.

There is a widespread rumour, still circulated, no doubt, by
members of the B.N.P. and/or the Roman Catholic church, that
eighty per cent or more of the people of Lesotho are Roman
Catholics. I don't know how these statistics have been computed,
but I know they are wrong. The Christian Council of Lesotho is
composed of representatives of all the churches in Lesotho, and
their representation is proportionate to that of their members.
On this board, there are seven Roman Catholics, six members of
the Lesotho Evangelical Church, five Anglicans and three who
represent pentecostal churches and all others. By my reckoning,
that would indicate that no more than one-third of the Basotho
are Roman Catholics, fewer if you count non-Christians and
non-believers. Hostility and competition among these Christian
churches have been fierce since the days of the missionaries.
This affected my life as an Anglican at a Roman Catholic school.

Every night we had to say the Hail Mary and turn off the lights
at half past nine. One evening, after the lights had been switched
off, Mary, a friend of mine who was not afraid to be seen with me,
came to my bed and whispered to me, 'The sister has told me that
when we are singing the song, "Oho Maria", when it comes to the
part where we sing, "we trust you", you are always singing, *"they
trust you".* Is that true?'

I said, 'It's funny, because one sister sits right at the back and
the other sits right at the front. I am in the middle. They are not
near me; they can't hear what I sing. I'm surprised that they can
make such an accusation.'

'But is it true?'

I said, 'No. It is not true. I have never sung the hymn any way
but the same way that everyone else sings it. Besides, I am a
Christian. I belong to the Anglican church and we believe most of
the same things that the Roman Catholics believe. We are not so
different.'

Mary whispered again, 'I was puzzled. I wondered if it was true. Because I thought you were a Christian and I knew that the nuns could not hear you singing.'

I whispered back, 'Look, even though we have so much confidence in these nuns, we can see that they are not so holy after all. They are just human beings, like us, because here is a nun who is telling a lie.'

She said, 'I am satisfied. This nun just wanted to slander your name. But you must be careful. You can see that they want to expel you from school.'

After that night, I tried to be quiet, because I was afraid to be expelled. I liked school very much and I had dreams for myself. I didn't want to work as a domestic servant, like my mother. I saw how that work made her old before her time and how her employers treated her like an animal. I was passing well in school. I knew that once you have been expelled from one high school, you will not be accepted at another; they ask for testimonials, and you will not get one if you are expelled. So I tried to keep quiet, no matter what was said about *Ntate* Mokhehle and the B.C.P. after that.

After *Ntate* Mookho had left, the sisters used to tell us to dissociate ourselves from the B.C.P., and they would look right at me and repeat what *Ntate* Mookho had said. I would keep silent, and my heart would pound very hard.

At one point the white sisters decided to expel me anyway. One black sister stood up against that decision. During her English lesson, she talked to us about apartheid and the Sharpeville Massacre in South Africa, and how it influenced affairs in Lesotho. She said that we must realize that the white sisters did not want the liberation of black people. They supported apartheid, and they came to Lesotho with a sense of their own martyrdom, ready to work with the 'downtrodden', but not willing to help us rise up and stand on our own feet. For them to feel good, it was necessary for us to remain 'downtrodden'. The white nuns felt they were protected by the British in our country and they didn't want us to become independent, because in a way they were afraid of us. They thought all the Basotho men wanted to marry them.

We giggled at that idea, but the black nun's statements really made sense to us. When the white sisters had talked about the Sharpeville Massacre, they were spiteful, telling us that Africans were foolish to think that they could fight white people. They said what happened at Sharpeville would happen anywhere that black people tried to fight whites. They had no sympathy for the blacks who were killed.

Despite my attempts to keep silent, I was once expelled, and my Uncle had to fight for me to be accepted back into the school. Most of my friends at school were told by the sisters to avoid me; the sisters said I was 'pro-communism'. I survived because I was hardworking and an above-average student and some of my friends could see through the lies and deceit of the white nuns.

I had begun to be defensive of my family's politics, and, during the next school year, I found a new boyfriend who led me even deeper into politics. This one came from Berea District and was working in the factories of South Africa, in the steel works. He was really serious; he was older than I, and he even wanted to marry me, but I told him, 'No, I want to finish my education and acquire a profession.'

I liked this boy because he liked politics; he knew something about life and he had ideas – perhaps because he was living in South Africa, where so much was going on. It was his letter about the Sharpeville Massacre in 1960 that almost got me thrown out of school.

There was no way for us to communicate except by the regular mail, which the sisters censored before they gave it to us. He sent me some press clippings after the Sharpeville Massacre, to show me what the papers were saying about it, and he wrote about how black people had been unfairly treated under apartheid. The white sisters could not tolerate this, because they did not want us to know much about politics and they clearly sided with the whites in South Africa anyway.

When this letter came, the Principal sister read it first, before giving it to me. I knew something was wrong by the look on her face when she called my name after supper that evening. She stood in front of us and called out, 'Hilda Chakela.'

I approached, trembling slightly with both fear and excitement.

'Come and see me in the office. Now.'

Normally, if a girl had received an improper letter, the sister would tell her to come to the office the next day. But this was clearly urgent. After lecturing me on the subject of boyfriends, she told me she was going to report to *Ntate* Charles, who was paying my school fees, that I was receiving letters from people who were involved in politics.

This gave me no real worries. My Uncle Charles was involved in politics much more than I was, so I knew he wouldn't mind about the politics. And he didn't. He did, however, ask me about the fellow who wrote the letter, and he told me, 'Look, if you have boyfriends, I don't want you to run about with them. Should you fall pregnant, they might refuse you. So let them come here to see you so I can know them.'

All my schoolmates and classmates were used to visiting me at home. Uncle Charles didn't mind the visits; he only minded my having friends whom he hadn't met. He wanted to know who their families were, too.

There were times when I felt trapped by all this supervision both at home and at school, and that's why I used to make excuses sometimes, lies, so I could go to meet my boyfriend. There was never any risk of my becoming pregnant, because even the boys of our time knew how to restrain themselves, and certainly the girls, who had so much more at risk, knew how to behave.

Our favourite writing exercises were secret letters to our boyfriends and although we used our history books to hide our boyfriends' photographs, we did occasionally become enthusiastic about academic work. We had to read many famous British writers, many plays by Shakespeare and Dickens' *A Tale of Two Cities* (which inspired me politically). We were not reading African writers; we were not even told that Africans were capable of writing novels or plays. I loved reading and I also read many books which I found at my uncle's house. At my uncle's I also found South African newspapers and magazines, like *Zonk* and *Drum*, and *The African*, which was highly political. I read so much from those papers and magazines that I knew all about *Ntate* Nelson Mandela, *Ntate* Oliver Tambo and others. I knew about all the political upheavals of South Africa. But we were taught nothing of politics at Holy Family.

I wanted to be like my mother's cousins, four sisters, all of them nurses. They were models to me, especially the elder one, who married a graduate of Fort Hare University. The man she married was a teacher in Lesotho, at Basutoland High School; from there he went to Zambia when it became independent; he also taught in Ghana; and he came to Swaziland for his last years of teaching. With all these travels, my mother's cousin continued to work as a nurse wherever they lived. To me they seemed sophisticated; they were living the way I wanted to live. Their children were brilliant, well looked after, well loved and (what impressed me most) both husband and wife played tennis. I saw them when I was young because each time they had a holiday, they came home to visit the wife's family in Ficksburg or the husband's family in Parys, the township of Tumahole. I dreamed of being like that – having important work to do, having beautifully-dressed children who are outstanding in school and going out to play tennis with my handsome, successful husband.

Most of the white nuns were good to us, in a condescending way. But there were two black nuns who were totally against apartheid, and they, like my mother's cousins, served as models to me of strong African women, even within a system which indoctrinated them to submit to authority. They used to have sessions with us, to tell us that the system of government in South Africa was bad. They told us that was why some South Africans sent their children to Lesotho to get an education. Sister Mary Antoinette taught us commercial arithmetic. Sister Mary Joseph taught us English, and, once we were successful in staging our first political action, bookkeeping and commerce.

It was in this struggle for a bookkeeping and commerce course that I discovered my leadership abilities. Our Latin teacher was a reverend father who came from Italy, but he was not a good teacher. We could notice that he was drinking – we could smell liquor on his breath, his speech was slurred, and he used to be rude to us. He would talk to us as if we knew Latin already; he would say things he knew we could not understand, just to embarrass us, and we knew he was laughing at us. We feared to think what he was saying to us.

We reported this to Sister Mary Joseph and told her that we felt that the school was being unfair to us. We wanted to learn something that we could practise when we left school. We were wasting our time in this Latin class. We wanted to do bookkeeping and commerce, and we asked whether there was any teacher who could teach that.

She advised us to write a letter to Mother Superior, who was a white lady from Belgium. We asked for a meeting to explain our case. Somehow I happened to be the spokesperson for our group; it was one girl from Johannesburg, named Agatha, and I, who came up with the suggestion for the new course. Sister Mary Joseph coached us on how to talk respectfully but persuasively to the Mother Superior and we managed to convince her that Latin was no longer useful; it was outdated; we could not get employment with it.

So the Reverend Father Thomas was told that Holy Family girls were no longer going to do Latin; they were going to do commerce and bookkeeping. When the boys at Sacred Heart were informed, they said they, too, wanted bookkeeping and commerce, and not Latin. That was how bookkeeping and commerce started at both schools – because the boys, too, did not want this *Ntate* from Italy. The boys even got to do typing, because the Brothers were rich and could afford typewriters. The Italian Father stopped teaching; we told them we didn't even want him to teach catechism; and we succeeded. After that he just did parish work. Sister Mary Joseph had secretly coached us through the whole process of making this change.

Later, when some students were failing bookkeeping and commerce, they would point to us and say, 'You know, Hilda and Agatha, it is your fault we are having these troubles. We would not be taking these courses if it were not for you.' They pretended to be angry with us, but we knew that we had led a movement that was important to them, and we had won. It was our first taste of success.

I felt that these two black nuns were motherly people who really wanted to teach us how to survive – how to restrain our anger, how we might sometimes have to ignore provocative words directed at us, and how nonetheless we had to stand up and fight for justice. There would be some things we could change, and we should try through prayer and negotiation to change them; but in life, we cannot immediately make change come. Sister Mary Joseph said, 'You can even think that God has forgotten about you. When you go out into the field to work, even when you are working with people of your own colour, you can be ill-treated. You should always be humble or indifferent towards the things you cannot change. Still, you should not forget to pray all the time and to work for change where change is necessary.' Sister taught us to be Christian revolutionaries and to listen to the inner voice. She said that when the time is right to take action, there will always be an inner voice that says, 'I have the courage. I have to speak out about this. I have to change this.'

Even now, I still love Sister Mary Joseph. She is a Mother Superior at a home for nuns in Berea District. She is very humble, very kind. Sometimes some nuns of high rank can be quite arrogant, but she isn't like that. She always wanted her girls to succeed. Even when we were working in offices in Maseru, she did not forget about us. She used to visit us and ask, 'How do you find your work? Are you improving yourself educationally?'

I felt her concern; that it was genuine. Even now, when I am older than she was when we started our small revolution to overturn Latin studies, I know that she is still watching me, wishing me well and praying for me to succeed. I am still one of 'her girls'.

I finished high school and passed well, but unfortunately Sister Mary Joseph wasn't able to protect me from the wrath of the white sisters, who gave me an unfavourable recommendation. They said I was 'too politically-minded and aggressive'. I did not get admission to King Edward Nursing School. That was a turning-point for me.

I knew I had been labelled 'politically-minded' both because my family was associated with the B.C.P. and because there had been a time when I had answered back to Ntate Mookho. But I had not really been politically active. When the white nuns blocked my way into nursing school, that was the point at which I decided that I would become politically active and that I would remain politically active for the rest of my life. I felt that I might as well speak up and tell the truth, and sing my own words to those hymns, whatever the consequences; because even when I kept quiet and sang the same words as everybody else, I was still going to be ostracised and punished. I think it was the example of Sister Mary Joseph, coupled with the behaviour of those white nuns, more than my family's association with the B.C.P. or my working-class boyfriend's instruction, that led me to become truly 'politically-minded'.

Basali!
A Photographic Essay

K. LIMAKATSO KENDALL

These *basali* enjoy an outside drama
staged in Mafeteng by Lesotho Theatre for
AIDS Education in February 1993.

'M'e 'M'aanna is a shrine-builder. She lives
alone in a small masonite house and
creates shrines to Catholic fathers with
clay, bottle caps, sticks, bits of broken
glass and candles. She lives a liturgical
life, praying and singing at her shrines at
regular hours daily. Many villagers
regard her eccentricity as proof that she is
a witch, and once her house was burnt to
the ground by witch-hunters.

'M'e 'M'anthabiseng Kori supports four of her seven children and three grandchildren by working as a gardener at the National University of Lesotho. Her husband took another wife while working in the mines of South Africa and no longer supports his first family.

JIVING! 'Jiving' can express defiance as well as joy. These little girls, who live in village houses without electricity, save their money to buy batteries for the casette/radio which is the source of their jive music. They seem to enjoy traditional Basotho music, disco, soul, and American country-western music equally.

'M'e 'M'alebohang lives alone in this clay
house she built with her own hands in
1980. She left her husband long ago
because he beat her; she has lost touch
with her only child.

African Gothic: *'M'e* 'M'alebohang and some neighbouring girls in her front garden.

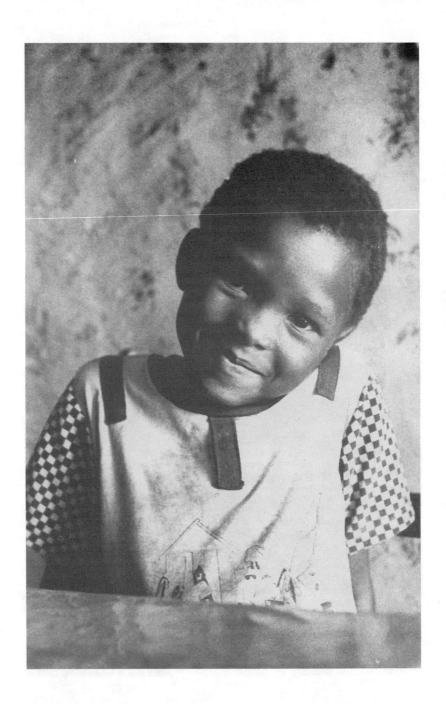

Lebohang's mother works as a maid for
a white family in Johannesburg; since her
grandmother's death in 1993 Lebohang
has lived with extended family members
who care for her in her mother's absence.

These three sisters live at Ha Tobu,
high on a hill overlooking the Roma Valley.

Glossary

abuti:	brother, young man.
Ao! Batho!:	Oh! People! Often used as an exclamation of disgust.
ausi:	sister, young woman.
i-babalazi:	hangover.
chobeliso:	elopement.
doek:	the Afrikaans word for a woman's headscarf; also *tubu* or *tuku*.
hantle:	nice, nicely, well; *ke hantle*: fine.
ho lokile:	fine, OK.
huisie:	a square or rectangular traditional thatch-roofed house.
joala:	home-made beer.
kannete!:	Truly!
khotso:	peace; also a greeting, *Khotso!*
koloi:	any vehicle; a bus, car, truck, etc.
kubu:	whip.
lekoerekoere:	a black African from outside southern Africa; pl., *makoerekoere*.
letsoalo:	fright.
lihalofote:	co-operative work in which the owner shares with the worker in the harvest.
likhomo tsa ho nyala:	bride-price.
litaola:	divining bones.
lobola:	bride-price; money or cattle paid by the groom's family to the bride's family.
lumela:	the most common greeting; literally it means, 'do you agree?'; in practice it means 'hello'.
Maburu:	Boers.
mahlanya:	mad people; *bayahlanya*: they are mad.

maloti:	unit of Basotho currency. One maloti is equal to one South African rand.
mangoane:	a mother's younger sister.
matekatse:	harlots, prostitutes.
Maxhosa:	Xhosa-speaking people.
'm'e:	literally, mother; a term of respect for any mature woman.
mokhoro:	a small hut.
molamu:	a large stick which can. be a walking-stick or a weapon.
moroho:	green, usually leafy, vegetables.
moroko:	dregs from home-made beer.
mosali:	woman; pl. *basali*.
motoho:	non-alcoholic drink made from ground sorghum.
motsoalle:	a very close friend.
naheng:	open fields for grazing.
ngalile:	a wife running away from her husband to her parents.
ngoanan'a moroetsana:	a grown-up girl.
ngoan'eso:	my dear.
ngoetsi:	daughter-in-law.
nkhono:	grandmother.
nyopa katala:	a barren woman in Sesotho folklore.
ntate:	father; a term of respect for any mature man.
ntsetse:	a word used when addressing a mother.
nyanyalea:	have fun.
o shobetse:	she has eloped.
padkos:	something to eat during the journey.
papa:	maize meal and water, cooked into a thick porridge; (usually served with milk, vegetables, egg, or, on festive occasions, meat).
papa mplothe:	a mixture of maize meal and water, served without anything else.
papasane:	a wild vegetable which is resistant to winter's cold.

patsi:	firewood.
phofo:	meal (usually maize meal); *phofo ea poone*, maize meal; *phofo ea koro*, wheat meal; *phofo ea mabele*, sorghum meal.
potlololo!:	*literally* shrink; used to convey embarrassment.
rakhali:	aunt.
rondavel:	a round, traditional thatch-roofed house.
sekhukhuni:	guerilla; freedom fighter.
seshoeshoe:	a dark cloth with a white print design, made in England; introduced by missionaries, but so popular among Basotho women since the turn of the century that it has come to be regarded as their 'traditional' dress. The name is derived from that of a Sotho king, Moshoeshoe.
sjambok:	whip.
thethana:	skirt of beads or string worn by young girls.
thithiboea:	a hairy centipede.
tsotsi:	a gangster or crook. pl. *tsotsis*.
tubu or *tuku*:	a headscarf or headwrap; also *doek*.
uena:	you.

Contributors

MOROESI AKHIONBARE was born in Maseru in 1945. She attended a Catholic girls' high school and studied towards a liberal arts degree in biology in the United States. Moroesi now works as Cultural Affairs Assistant with the United States Information Service in Maseru. This prose-poem in the form of a letter is addressed to her maternal grandmother who reared her and whom, in accordance with Basotho tradition, she knew as 'M'e, or mother.

HILDA 'M'AMAPELE CHAKELA was born in 1944 in the district of Leribe. Her South African mother became a domestic servant in order to support her children. 'M'amapele grew up being shuttled from her mother's family in South Africa to her father's politically active family in Lesotho. This story is a part of her unpublished autobiography, told to K. Limakatso Kendall, written down and shaped by Kendall, and re-written by the two of them together.

GUGULETHU S. DLAMINI was born in 1967 in Durban, South Africa, but received her higher education in Lesotho at the National University of Lesotho. Before that she trained as a teacher and taught at Mafu High School, Bergville, Natal for a year. She now works in Durban. This story was told to Gugu in Zulu by a woman who wishes to remain anonymous. Gugu translated the story into English, trying to remain true to the language but taking some liberties in rearranging paragraphs and the order of the telling.

K. LIMAKATSO KENDALL teaches drama at the University of Natal. In 1992–94 she was a Fulbright Scholar from the U.S.A. in the English Department at the National University of Lesotho. She is a single mother who has worked as a waitress, house painter, secretary, actress, counsellor, and freelance writer on her way to becoming an academic. This background informs her enthusiasm for working-class women's voices.

SR. ALINA KHABANE entered the congregation of the Sisters of Charity in 1956. She now teaches at Paray High School in Thaba-Tseka, deep in the heartland of rural Lesotho. 'Arriving Home in a Helicopter' is an autobiographical story told to Sr. Alina in Sesotho by her sister-in-law, Julia 'M'amatseliso Khabane. Sr. Alina very carefully preserved the language, especially its rural idiomatic expressions, which Julia used in her original telling.

MAPHELEBA LEKHETHO left his home village, Mosenekeng, at the age of six and went to Tsoelike, where he grew up in his aunt's household. He now teaches at Sefikeng High School in Teyateyaneng District. This story was told to Mapheleba by his aunt 'M'akena, his surrogate mother. He listened to her telling parts of the story as he was growing up, and then more recently he asked her to tell him the whole story again.

'M'ATSELENG LENTSOENYANE worked for ten years as a primary school teacher. In her childhood she used to listen to her great-grandmother telling stories, and she herself developed the habit. She often tells stories to her three daughters and her husband, sometimes in Sesotho and sometimes in English. 'Why Blame Her?' is a story about the life of one of the author's age-mates.

CLEMENT MOIKETSI MATJELO was born at Sekubu, Butha-Buthe, Lesotho in 1969. He completed his B.A. Ed. degree in 1993. 'What About the *Lobola*?' was told to Matjelo in Sesotho by a Mosotho woman who wishes to remain anonymous. Matjelo has translated her story into English without making editorial changes, carefully preserving the somewhat formal tone of her use of Sesotho.

NOMAKHOSI MNTUYEDWA was born in So-
phiatown, Johannesburg, in 1947. She attended
school in South Africa and Swaziland and obtained a B.A. degree from the University of
Botswana, Lesotho and Swaziland in 1971. She
now works as a freelance journalist and is living
in the U.S.A. with her family. This autobiographical short story is about her physical and moral
escape from South Africa.

MASEFINELA MPHUTHING is the fourth of
ten children, born on 19 June 1948, at a village
on a hilltop overlooking Hlotse. She completed
her B.A. at the National University of Lesotho in
1981 and her Master of Public Administration at
the University of Southern California in 1987.
She is now the Registrar at NUL, the first
woman ever to hold this post. This poem was
published in a journal and won prizes in the
U.S.A., and this is its first appearance in a book.

MZAMANE NHLAPO completed his O levels in
1981, the year his father died. He worked as a
miner in South Africa and went on to the
National University of Lesotho in 1989. He is
now principal of a secondary school in Mafeteng
District. 'Give Me a Chance' is constructed partly
from memory and partly from Nhlapo's trans-
lation of the story as told to him by his mother,
Mama KaZili, aged sixty, who is a teacher at
'Makong Primary School.

MPHO 'M'ATSEPO NTHUNYA was born in Lesotho in 1930 and spent much of her youth in Benoni Location, where she learned to speak seven languages in addition to her native Sesotho. She returned to Lesotho in 1949, and lived in the Maluti Mountains, rearing her children, raising sheep and growing crops. Just before her husband's death in 1969, she began to work at the National University of Lesotho as a cleaning woman.

'M'AMOROOSI 'M'ASEELE MARTHA QACHA was born on 31 August 1966. This is her first published story, and she says she thought she had no talent for writing until she joined a women's writing group in Maseru and felt inspired and encouraged by other Basotho women. She thanks her parents, who gave her an education; her husband, Mokuoane Qacha, for his support; and her daughters, for being there.

MONICA NTHABELENG RAMAROTHOLE is the fifth daughter in her family. Her parents divorced at the time she was born, leaving her in the care of a grandmother who felt imposed upon and could not support her. Monica's mother gave her home-schooling up to the secondary-school level. Now a graduate of the National University of Lesotho, Monica works in gender research and community development, and she plans to continue writing. 'The African Goddess', an autobiographical story, is her first.

This is an autobiographical story by TEMBELA SELEKE. Tembela left Transkei (South Africa) in 1981 to join her husband, who was in Lesotho as a refugee and was assassinated during the 1982 December massacre by the South African Defence Force (SADF). After her mourning period, she procured work, remarried, and later, in 1989, decided to further her studies at the National University of Lesotho. She has now returned to South Africa to live.

MPINE TENTE is presently the Principal Secretary for the Ministry of Information and Broadcasting of the Kindgom of Lesotho. She holds a B.A. Ed. degree and a postgraduate diploma in mass communication. She is a single parent who says she likes to work with male colleagues as partners, so long as they respect her views as she does theirs. 'Ask Him to Explain' is an autobiographical story.

INAHANENG TSEKANA was born in 1965 in the Mokhotlong district, where he went to work as a herdboy at the age of seven. He now teaches at Adventville High School in Maseru. 'How She Lost Her Eye' is a true story which was told to Inahaneng in Sesotho by his Aunt Sehlahla. Some of the names in the story have been changed to save embarrassment.